MEDITERRANEAN DIET (FOR BEGINNERS:

Set Sail on a Tasty Journey of Delicious and Healthy Dishes | Rediscover Yourself Thanks to the Intangible Cultural Heritage of the Mare Nostrum Recipes | Pegasus Method

Copyright © 2023

Sarah Roslin

COPYRIGHT & DISCLAIMER: all rights are reserved by law. No part of this book may be reproduced without the authors' written permission. It is expressly forbidden to transmit this book to others, neither in paper or electronic format, neither for money nor free of charge. What is reported in this book is the result of years of studies and accumulated experience. The achievement of the same results is not guaranteed. The reader assumes full responsibility for their choices. The book is exclusively for educational purposes.

TABLE OF CONTENTS

1 INTRODUCTION

The Mediterranean Diet, a widely recognized and healthy dietary pattern, offers numerous benefits for overall well-being. Characterized by its high consumption of fruits, vegetables, and whole grains and low levels of saturated fat and cholesterol, the diet primarily emphasizes plant-based foods, with moderate meat and dairy intake. As stated by the Centers for Disease Control and Prevention (CDC), the Mediterranean Diet is linked to a reduced risk of heart disease, stroke, chronic conditions such as obesity and type 2 diabetes, certain cancers, and premature death.

At the core of the Mediterranean Diet are abundant fruits, vegetables, whole grains, nuts, legumes, olive oil, fish, seafood, moderate red wine consumption (if desired), and minimal processed food intake. These nutrient-dense foods provide essential vitamins and minerals for optimal health, while maintaining low calorie counts and minimal unhealthy fats or sugars.

The Mediterranean diet's health benefits stem from its rich supply of antioxidants found in fruits, vegetables, and whole grains, which protect cells from damage and help prevent chronic diseases. Furthermore, the diet's low fat and saturated fat content reduces the risk of heart disease and other health issues.

Not only is the Mediterranean diet healthful, but it is also affordable. A study published in The Lancet revealed that individuals adhering to the Mediterranean diet were more likely to afford high-quality, nutritious food, making it more accessible than other dietary patterns.

Distinct from many other diets, the Mediterranean diet does not impose a lengthy list of restrictions. Instead, it emphasizes wholesome eating and encourages physical and social activities to maintain a healthy heart and mind for years to come.

The long life spans of Mediterranean people can be attributed to their dietary habits, which this book will explore in detail. Throughout the book, you'll find essential information about the diet's fundamentals, as well as an array of inspiring and delicious recipes to try.

1.1 What is a Mediterranean Diet?

The Mediterranean diet is a wholesome, balanced eating plan inspired by the traditional diets of countries in the Mediterranean region, such as Greece, Italy, Spain, and Cyprus. These countries have long-standing histories of healthy living. The Mediterranean diet has proven effective in reducing the risk of heart disease, stroke, and other chronic illnesses.

This dietary pattern, typically consumed in Mediterranean Sea regions, consists of fruits, vegetables, nuts, beans, whole grains, and moderate amounts of meat and dairy products. It has been associated with a decreased risk of heart disease, stroke, and certain types of cancer.

There are several reasons why the Mediterranean diet contributes to better health. Firstly, the antioxidants in fruits and vegetables help protect the body against diseases. Secondly, the diet's high fiber and low sugar content aids in maintaining a healthy weight. Thirdly, the variety of nutrients in the Mediterranean diet ensures the body receives all essential vitamins and minerals. Lastly, incorporating more plant-based foods can help increase satiety and reduce overall appetite, making it an environmentally friendly, delicious, and healthier choice.

If you're seeking a nutritious and sustainable way of eating that also offers a wide array of flavors, the Mediterranean diet is an excellent choice.

1.2 The History of the Mediterranean Diet

The Mediterranean diet has long been a topic of discussion and a source of pride for those living around the Mediterranean region. Throughout history, this area has been central to many defining moments of human civilization, from the rise of the Greeks and the Roman conquest to the westward expansion of the Persians, the Crusades in the 10th century, and the subsequent colonization of the New World by European nations.

Efforts to promote the diet date back centuries. As early as the 1600s, Giacomo Castelvetro published a book in England in 1614 describing fruits, vegetables, and herbs used in Italian cooking, which he suggested could be incorporated into English cuisine. In the late 19th century, locals in the Mediterranean region attempted to teach incoming immigrants about the importance of the Mediterranean diet for health and well-being.

During this time, European immigration to the American colonies contributed to the spread of the Mediterranean diet to the West. The establishment of the New England Kitchen, initially intended to reinforce Yankee cooking culture and Americanize poor immigrants, had an unexpected outcome. Rather than assimilating into Yankee cooking practices, the Mediterranean diet grew stronger and influenced the locals.

The New England Kitchen ultimately facilitated the distribution of food from California farms to major urban and immigration centers, allowing primarily Mediterranean groups to maintain their traditional diets. Historians believe that the delicious flavors of the Mediterranean diet encouraged people to abandon unhealthy foods in favor of fresh vegetables, fruits, grains, and olive oil, contributing to the diet's growing popularity.

This growth continued, bolstered by the ongoing quest to improve our understanding of nutrition, which led to numerous studies that further reinforced the value of the Mediterranean diet.

1.3 Who Is This Diet Suitable For?

One of the best aspects of the Mediterranean diet is that it is appropriate for everyone. Children, young adults, and the elderly can all benefit from the nutrient-dense foods that are essential to the Mediterranean diet. The Mediterranean diet is excellent since it is neither restricted nor rigid. It is a way of life rather than a diet. As a result, it allows everyone to join and enjoy the colorful and diverse array of Mediterranean-style cuisine that comprise it. So you may involve your entire family in this new way of eating. In reality, mealtimes are an experience where complete multigenerational families traditionally spend time together and bond in Mediterranean towns and villages. Transitioning from high-fat and sugary ready meals in front of the television to healthy meals served at the dinner table can transform your family life while also providing considerable health benefits to all members of your family.

Even better, you can follow the Mediterranean diet at home, work, or school. Pack the kids a great Greek salad for lunch, or make some falafel flatbreads to take to a park picnic. Your family and friends will be grateful to you for exposing them to this great way of eating.

1.4 The Food Pyramid of the Mediterranean Diet

The Mediterranean diet is a healthy eating plan that emphasizes fruits, vegetables, whole grains, and fish. It is based on the principle that a diet rich in fruits and vegetables, moderate in proteins, and low in saturated fats results in numerous health benefits. The food pyramid of the Mediterranean diet serves as a visual representation of this eating plan, consisting of six sections: fruits, vegetables, grains, oils, salt, and dairy. The Mediterranean Diet food pyramid has five tiers, providing a guide for choosing what to put on your plate. These tiers are as follows:

- **Tier 1**: Regular Social and Physical Activities
  That's right, the biggest tier in the pyramid is dedicated not to food but to relationships with others and with yourself.
- **Tier 2**: Vegetables, Fruit, Whole Grains, Beans, Legumes, Seeds, Nuts, Herbs, Spices, and Olive oil. The bulk on your plate should consist mostly of vegetables, with the rest sprinkled on top. In layman's terms, go green with a rainbow of colors on top. This is a stark contrast to the typical Western diet, which consists mostly of red meat and starchy sides.
- **Tier 3**: Fish and Seafood
  If you feel the need to eat meat, then always choose seafood first, especially wild-caught fish. In the diet, fish should be served at least twice a week.
- **Tier 4**: Eggs, Yogurt, Cheese, and Poultry
  Eggs and dairy products can be enjoyed regularly in the Mediterranean diet, but it is emphasized that they should only be served in small portions.
- **Tier 5**: Meat and Sweets
  Meat does not play a central role in the Mediterranean diet, as farm animals are rarely slaughtered except on special occasions. If meat is served, it should be accompanied by plenty of vegetables. Sweets are also reserved for special occasions, ideally enjoyed no more than once a week.

Initially, it may seem challenging to consistently purchase fresh whole foods, but planning ahead can simplify the process. Growing some of your own food, such as herbs and spices, can also be beneficial.

1.5 Specific Guidelines for Mediterranean Diet

The Mediterranean diet has established the following key guidelines for selecting foods to serve and consume in order to achieve the optimal benefits of this diet.

1.5.1 Go for Wholesome Fats

A Mediterranean diet is high in healthy fats, such as olive oil, nuts, and seeds, and low in saturated fats. These types of fats are essential for a healthy diet because they help reduce inflammation and protect the heart:

- Use olive oil or other healthy fats when frying food. These oils help preserve the vitamins and minerals that are lost when foods are cooked in non-Mediterranean oils.
- Use butter or ghee when roasting vegetables or meats. These fats impart a delicious flavor and help keep the food moist.
- Include nuts, seeds, or legumes as ingredients in Mediterranean dishes. These foods are high in fiber, essential fatty acids, and other nutrients that can enhance the overall healthfulness of your diet.

Nuts of various types, as well as canola oil, contain healthy lipids and linolenic acid. Linolenic acid is an omega-3 fatty acid. Omega-3 fatty acids are beneficial to one's health because they can reduce blood clotting, decrease the risk of a heart attack, lower triglyceride levels, maintain stable blood pressure, and strengthen blood vessels.

Fatty fish, which are commonly used in Mediterranean dishes, are also rich in omega-3 fatty acids. Examples of fatty fish include lake sardines, trout, herring, mackerel, albacore tuna, and salmon. The Mediterranean Sea is abundant with these fatty fish..

1.5.2 Go for Greens and Grains

If you're looking to follow a Mediterranean diet, make sure to add more greens and grains to your meals. Experts recommend at least six servings of colorful vegetables and two servings of whole grains each day. Here are some tips for incorporating these foods into your diet:

- Add a salad as a main course or side dish: A salad is a great way to get loads of nutrients and fiber while switching up your routine. Choose fruits, vegetables, and lean protein sources like grilled chicken or fish instead of processed foods.
- Start your day with a fiber-rich breakfast: A bowl of oatmeal with nuts, seeds, and berries is a great way to start the day. Add in some yogurt or milk for added benefits.
- Snack on fresh fruits and vegetables: Keep your snacks healthy by opting for fresh fruits and vegetables instead of processed snacks. Grab some grapes, figs, carrots, or apples instead of chips or candy bars.

1.5.3 Drink Red Wine in Moderation

The Mediterranean diet is a heart-healthy way of eating that has been linked with reduced rates of heart disease, stroke, and some types of cancer. One key component of the Mediterranean diet is the consumption of red wine, which has been shown to have health benefits. However, like any other alcoholic drink, red wine should be consumed in moderation. Here are guidelines for how much red wine to enjoy on a Mediterranean diet:

- If you choose to enjoy a glass or two of red wine as part of your Mediterranean diet, aim to drink no more than one glass per day for women and up to two glasses per day for men. For people who don't drink alcohol, there is no need to start; you can still enjoy the benefits of a Mediterranean diet without alcohol.
- If you are trying to cut back on your alcohol intake, start by swapping out one glass of red wine for a cup of herbal tea or water. If you find that you are still craving a glass of red wine, then consider going for a lower-calorie option like an iced tea or unsweetened cranberry juice instead.
- If you are pregnant or breastfeeding, it is best to avoid drinking alcohol altogether. Pregnant women should not consume alcohol, as it can pose risks to the baby's health. Breastfeeding mothers should also be cautious about alcohol consumption, as it can pass through breast milk to the baby. Consult with your healthcare provider for personalized advice on alcohol consumption during pregnancy and breastfeeding.

1.5.4 Sharing Meals Together

One of the most important components of this diet plan is that it emphasizes the social parts of your life. It recognizes that humans are social animals who need to spend time with others. Even if you are an introvert who prefers not to spend all of your time in loud, noisy, and busy places, it is still necessary for you to engage in some social interaction on a regular basis. This diet plan requires you to learn how to eat at least one meal a day with your family. And this should be made a huge deal. Rather than sitting down and preparing dinner in five minutes, make at least one of your meals a great occasion that everyone can enjoy. Even if you only start with one meal each week, this will make a difference. If you can set aside an hour or more each week to prepare this meal, you will be able to work on strengthening your bonds with others in your family. Enjoy your dinner, talk to others, share tales and knowledge, and tell them about your day. This is a terrific way to calm down in this fast-paced world, reconnect, and may do incredible things for your stress levels and happiness. Begin with one or two slow and leisurely meals with your family, and then go to adding more social activities to your life. This does not have to be stressful, and it should not be. Consider meeting a buddy for coffee, having a play date at the park, or doing something else that gets you out of the house while still allowing you to connect with others and have a pleasant time.

1.5.5 The Importance of Physical Exercise

When following a Mediterranean diet, it is important to get enough physical activity. The recommended amount of exercise for a person of any age is 150 minutes per week. However, people following a Mediterranean diet should aim for at least 225 minutes per week of moderate-intensity aerobic activity or 75 minutes per week of vigorous-intensity aerobic activity. This amount of exercise can be achieved by participating in a variety of activities, such as walking, cycling, swimming, and playing tennis. In addition to getting the recommended amount of exercise, it is also important to make sure that the physical activity is done in a healthy way. This means that the exercise should be moderate-intensity and include a mix of aerobic and anaerobic activity. Aerobic activity includes activities such as walking, running, and swimming; anaerobic activity includes activities such as biking, weightlifting, and football.

1.5.6 Learning How to Manage Your Stress

Stress is one of the biggest factors that can prevent people from sticking to their diets. The Mediterranean diet is known to be helpful in controlling stress levels, so it's important to follow some guidelines if you want to stick to this diet while under pressure. For starters, try to relax before meals by taking a few minutes for yourself. Eat slowly and focus on the taste and texture of your food. Alternatively, try aromatherapy – many people find that scents such as lavender or lemon help to calm them down before eating. Secondly, make sure you have plenty of water and non-caffeinated drinks with you when you're on the go. When you're stressed, your body releases cortisol – a hormone that can increase your appetite and make it harder to stick to your diet. Avoid caffeine close to meals if possible, as it will only make things worse. Finally, stay positive and remind yourself why you're doing this. If you find yourself getting frustrated or tempted by unhealthy foods, remember why you decided to start following the Mediterranean diet in the first place. This way, you'll be more likely to stick to your plan no matter what happens. As you can see, the Mediterranean diet is not just about you working on the foods that you consume. Instead, it is all about changing the way that you live your lifestyle. Many times, Americans are going to feel stressed out and tired because they have too much going on. They don't slow down and spend time with those who matter. They don't even slow down to enjoy their meal. They are moving fast, doing too much work, and they are just not happy with their quality of life.

The Mediterranean diet is a great way to improve your health. Not only does it promote a healthy weight, but it also contains antioxidants, fiber, and other nutrients that can help prevent disease. If you're looking for a healthy eating plan that's also easy to follow, the Mediterranean diet may be the perfect fit for you.

1.6 Tips for Eating Out On a Mediterranean Diet

When dining out on a Mediterranean diet, it is important to keep in mind some tips and tricks. Here are four simple tips to follow:

- Order fresh fruits and vegetables as your main course instead of meat. This will help you stay on track with your dietary goals and fill up on healthy nutrients.
- Try to avoid eating high-calorie items like dessert or bread. Stick to low-fat versions or choose a dish with grilled or roasted chicken as the main protein source.
- Whenever possible, order wine or water instead of sugary drinks. These drinks can spike your blood sugar levels and make it harder to stick to your diet overall.
- Take advantage of the Mediterranean diet's emphasis on whole grains, legumes, and nuts. These foods provide fiber, protein, and other nutrients that can boost your health overall.

2 UNDERSTANDING THE SCIENCE BEHIND THE MEDITERRANEAN DIET

Since Dr. Ancel Keys, the Minnesota-based physiologist who extolled the virtues of the Mediterranean diet about fifty years ago, more evidence has emerged demonstrating that there are beneficial effects to be obtained by consuming a diet based on a high intake of fresh fruits and vegetables, whole grains, fish, and moderate amounts of liquor on a regular basis. The Mediterranean diet, when combined with regular physical activity and quitting smoking, can reduce 80 percent of coronary heart disease, 70 percent of strokes, and 90 percent of Type 2 diabetes. One of the key reasons science supports this diet is that it has a greater fat intake. And the fact that it comes in the form of monounsaturated and polyunsaturated fats found in olive oil, which lower triglyceride levels while increasing HDL or "good cholesterol," makes it even better. There is scientific evidence that the Mediterranean diet not only reduces the risk of heart disease but also of other ailments and diseases such as Alzheimer's and cancer. The evidence is not only empirical but also the result of several rounds of research and numerous studies on the efficacy of consuming a diet patterned after the Southern Mediterranean lifestyle, the results of which have unequivocally confirmed what was already known - that the Mediterranean diet is the real thing. It works, and it is far superior to any drug developed with the goal of improving your health and extending your life. The benefit of this diet is that it may be followed and benefited from at any stage of life. It is not only a fantastic strategy to prevent disease, but it is also a good approach to lower the risk factors associated with heart disease. A study conducted by the University of Barcelona on patients with risk factors such as obesity, smoking, and diabetes established this unambiguously. They were divided into three groups, one of which was given a low-fat diet and the other two types of Mediterranean diet plans. The disparity in results gained from the two types of Mediterranean diets and the low-fat diet was so remarkable that the latter study had to be halted after five years! The incidence of heart attacks and strokes fell by 30% among those who followed Mediterranean diets. The low-fat diet was so bland and tasteless that scientists were forced to allow individuals to switch to their regular diet, which was significantly tastier due to its preponderance of red meat and commercially prepared food products. In the end, without reproducing the technical specifics of the several studies that unequivocally indicate that the Mediterranean diet is beneficial, one could make do by attributing it to a variety of obvious reasons. The most important reason is that it enhances longevity. Not just that, it comprehensively enhances your quality of life. Just look at the number of benefits that accrue to you by following this wonder diet:

- Makes your brain sharper and healthier
- Protects you against chronic diseases and helps fight cancer
- Lowers risk of heart disease by reducing blood pressure and "bad" cholesterol
- Defends you against diabetes
- Keeps depression at bay
- Helps you lose weight
- Protects you against Parkinson's disease
- Protects you against Alzheimer's disease
- It is good for arthritis
- Good for your dental health

3 THE POTENTIAL BENEFITS OF THE DIET

The Mediterranean diet is renowned for being full of healthy foods, such as fruits, vegetables, fish, lean meats, and nuts which makes it an excellent choice if you want to improve your physical and mental wellbeing.

3.1 Improves Hearth Health

The Mediterranean diet is a nutrient-rich, low-calorie diet that is associated with a lower incidence of heart disease. Some of the key nutrients found in the Mediterranean diet include:

- Omega-3 fatty acids: A rich source of omega-3 fatty acids can improve heart health by reducing the risk of arrhythmia and heart disease.
- Fiber: A source of soluble fiber can help to decrease bad cholesterol levels and improve blood sugar control.
- Vitamins and minerals: The Mediterranean diet is rich in vitamins and minerals, including potassium, magnesium, folate, and vitamin C, which are all important for heart health.

3.2 Aids In Weight Loss

When you want to lose weight, the Mediterranean diet is often recommended as one of the best ways to go. It's a diet that is high in fruits, vegetables, and whole grains, low in saturated fats and cholesterol, and moderate in protein. There is also a very large emphasis on leading a healthy and productive lifestyle while completely avoiding any kind of processed foods. All of these together combined helps to lose weight in the long run and stay healthier.

3.3 Improves Your Outlook

The Mediterranean diet has been shown to improve your appearance in a number of ways. The rich nutrients and antioxidants in the foods help to reduce the look of wrinkles, age spots, and other signs of aging. In addition, the low levels of saturated fat and cholesterol in the diet help to improve your heart health. Finally, healthy portion sizes and frequent meals help to keep your calorie intake lower, which can help to reduce your weight.

3.4 Protects You Against Diseases

The Mediterranean diet, which is derived from the traditional food habits of people in the Mediterranean region, has been linked with a decreased risk of diseases such as heart disease, stroke, cancer, and Alzheimer's disease. The main components of the Mediterranean diet are fruits, vegetables, whole grains, legumes, and nuts, in addition to moderate amounts of fish and dairy products. The Mediterranean diet is believed to be beneficial because it is high in antioxidants and contains healthy fats.

3.5 Keeps Your Energy Levels Up

Logically, when you put higher-quality fuels into your body, then you will enjoy better performance from your body. The Mediterranean diet works on exactly this principle. By fuelling your body with fruits and vegetables, whole grains, and moderate quantities of fish, lean meats, and other protein sources, you can enjoy a boost in your energy levels. Your fatigue and sensations of sluggishness should be reduced, and you may also enjoy better quality sleep which will allow you to wake up each morning feeling completely rejuvenated.

4 MANY DISEASES THE DIET CAN FIGHT

While many people may start to look at the Mediterranean diet as a way to lose weight, it won't take long researching the diet or long being on a diet before you realize that it can help you in so many other ways as well. Countless different health benefits come from eating the way that the Mediterranean diet asks you to. You just need to decide that it is time to get started.

There are so many different health benefits that are going to show themselves when it comes to this diet plan that once you get started, you will wonder why you didn't decide to do it earlier. Some of the best health benefits, though certainly not the only ones, include:

4.1 Can Help Prevent Heart Disease

Heart disease is a leading cause of death in the United States, and it's responsible for more deaths than any other type of cancer. A healthy diet is one of the best ways to reduce your risk of heart disease, but it's not always easy to follow a healthy diet. One way to help make eating a healthy diet easier is to follow a Mediterranean diet.

The Mediterranean diet, which is heavy in fruits, vegetables, legumes, and nuts, has been shown to protect against heart diseases. The diet is low in saturated fats and cholesterol, and it emphasizes whole grains and low-fat dairy products.

There is mounting evidence that eating a Mediterranean-style diet can help protect against heart disease. The Mediterranean diet is rich in fruits, vegetables, and whole grains and low in saturated fat and cholesterol. These foods have been shown to reduce the risk of heart attack and stroke. In addition, the Mediterranean diet has been linked with a decreased risk of obesity, which also contributes to heart disease.

4.2 Can Help Cognition and Memory in Older Adults

Memory is a skill that declines with age, but the Mediterranean diet has been shown to improve memory in elders. The diet is high in fruits, vegetables, whole grains, and moderate amounts of wine. In addition, it is rich in omega-3 fatty acids and antioxidants. The benefits of the Mediterranean diet for memory are likely due to the variety of foods it includes as well as the antioxidants and other nutrients it contains. These nutrients may help protect against cognitive decline and Alzheimer's disease.

The Mediterranean Diet is high in antioxidants, which are believed to help protect the brain from damage caused by free radicals. Free radicals are molecules that can damage cells and cause inflammation. The antioxidants found in the Mediterranean Diet can help scavenge free radicals before they cause too much damage. Additionally, the Mediterranean Diet is high in monounsaturated fatty acids (MUFA), which have been shown to improve cognitive function in both young and old adults. In addition to reducing oxidative stress, MUFA has been linked with improved memory and cognitive function due to its role in improving blood flow to the brain. A study published in The Journals of Gerontology, Series B, found that those following a Mediterranean diet had better scores on tests of memory and cognitive function than those who followed a traditional American diet. The study assessed 116 older adults who were divided into two groups: one group followed a Mediterranean diet, and the other followed a typical American diet. The participants were assessed for their memory and cognitive function at baseline and again six months later. The Mediterranean group had significantly better scores on tests of memory and cognitive function than the American group at both time points. The researchers believe that the beneficial effects of the Mediterranean diet on memory may be due to its high levels of antioxidants, which have been shown to protect against brain damage and age-related cognitive decline. In addition, the lower levels of inflammation found in those following a Mediterranean diet may also contribute to improved memory function.

4.3 Can Lower Your Risk of Depression

You will also discover that this type of food plan is capable of improving more than just your memory. According to a recent study published in Molecular Psychiatry, there is a strong correlation between the

Mediterranean diet and a lower prevalence of depression. This was a massive study, but it was because it was an amalgamation of information from 41 distinct studies, four of which would look at the relationship between the Mediterranean diet and depression over time in over 37,000 adults. When these four studies were examined, it was discovered that those who followed this diet had a substantially lower risk of depression, up to 33% lower than those who followed alternative diets that did not compare to the Mediterranean diet at all. What this means for your health is that if you are suffering from depression or want to avoid it because you have a family history of the disease, following a Mediterranean diet may be the best option for you. The Mediterranean diet is a popular way of eating that has been linked with a lower incidence of cancer. Research has found that people who eat a Mediterranean diet are less likely to develop prostate, ovarian, and other cancers. Scientists aren't sure why the diet is protective, but they believe that it may be because of the high levels of antioxidants and fiber in foods on a diet.
However, This program is rich in fruits, vegetables, whole grains, and seafood and has been associated with a lower risk of cancer. The diet is thought to reduce the risk by promoting a healthy lifestyle that includes regular exercise and a healthy diet. Studies have also shown that the Mediterranean diet can help to reduce the growth of cancer cells.

4.4 Can Help You Fight Some Types of Cancer

The Mediterranean diet is a popular way of eating that has been linked with a lower incidence of cancer. Research has found that people who eat a Mediterranean diet are less likely to develop prostate, ovarian, and other cancers. Scientists aren't sure why the diet is protective, but they believe that it may be because of the high levels of antioxidants and fiber in foods on a diet. However, This program is rich in fruits, vegetables, whole grains, and seafood and has been associated with a lower risk of cancer. The diet is thought to reduce the risk by promoting a healthy lifestyle that includes regular exercise and a healthy diet. Studies have also shown that the Mediterranean diet can help to reduce the growth of cancer cells.

4.5 Can Help You to Fight Off Type 2 Diabetes

The Mediterranean diet is a diet that is high in healthy fats, low in processed foods, and rich in fruits and vegetables. Studies have shown that people who follow a Mediterranean diet are less likely to develop type 2 diabetes. This is because the Mediterranean diet is rich in healthy fats, which helps to prevent obesity and insulin resistance. Furthermore, the Mediterranean diet is also high in fruits and vegetables, which are antioxidants and contain nutrients that help to regulate blood sugar levels. The Mediterranean diet is a healthy way to eat that can help to prevent type 2 diabetes.

4.6 Can Help Reduce Inflammation

Inflammation is increasingly the silent cause of many chronic diseases. Arthritis is an inflammation of the joints caused by a multitude of factors, including purine-rich diets. Other inflammatory disorders cause discomfort to the soft tissues of the digestive tract. Endometriosis, a disorder characterized by inflammation of the uterine walls, is a particular source of concern among women. A study led by Dr. Tamer Seckin of the Endometriosis Foundation of America discovered that a Mediterranean-style diet could truly help cure or lessen the inflammation associated with endometriosis. This is primarily due to the inclusion of anti-inflammatory items in the diet. Overall, studies have demonstrated that a diet high in anti-inflammatory substances can reduce internal inflammation. This diet is also virtually fully gluten-free and free of processed foods, both of which are known inflammatory triggers.

4.7 Can Help You Fight Alzheimer's

Alzheimer's disease is a serious concern in many countries throughout the world since it is a disease that is rapidly spreading, yet we still don't know what causes it or how to cure it. Recent studies on the effects of the Mediterranean diet, on the other hand, may contribute to scientific advancements in this area. Patients who were advised to follow the Mediterranean diet showed "significant improvement in executive functioning in male participants vs. females who consumed a Mediterranean diet," according to Samantha Gardener, a Ph.D. candidate at Edith Cowan University in Western Australia. Gardener's study also claimed that the Mediterranean diet causes a "slowing of metabolic syndrome, kidney protection, and a lower risk of various chronic diseases." The study concludes, "our findings underline the importance of consuming a balanced diet in terms of reducing risk for cognitive decline and Alzheimer's disease." Of course, many more studies and studies will be needed to completely understand the process underlying Alzheimer's disease, but one thing is certain: a good diet is critical to overall health and even more so to brain health and the prevention of degenerative disorders. Perhaps it is no surprise that the elderly in Sicily continue to operate normally despite their senior age and can enjoy the benefits of a quiet and peaceful existence far into their golden years. If that's all in the diet, then there's a lot to be said about embracing healthy eating habits like those promoted by the Mediterranean diet.

5 MEDITERRANEAN DIET VS. OTHER PROGRAMS

The Mediterranean Diet, as would be evident by now, is not really a diet that has been thought up to address certain lifestyle or health-related issues. It is a name given to the lifestyle and dietary habits of villagers living in the Southern Mediterranean region over centuries. But now that it has been identified by premier nutritionists and medical authorities as being the panacea for all the ills that result from following the modern Western hedonistic lifestyle, it might not be remiss to stack it up with other well-heralded diets and see how it fares.

5.1 The DASH Diet vs. the Mediterranean Diet

The Mediterranean diet is a popular way of eating that emphasizes fruits, vegetables, whole grains, and nuts; it's also low in saturated fat and cholesterol. The DASH diet, on the other hand, is rich in fruits, vegetables, whole grains, and low-fat dairy products; it's also low in saturated fat and cholesterol. The two diets have many similarities. They both emphasize fresh foods and limit processed foods. Both diets are high in fiber and low in sugar. And both diets have been shown to be effective for weight loss. However, there are some differences between the two diets. The Mediterranean diet is more balanced than the DASH diet. The DASH diet is high in protein and low in carbs, which can lead to weight gain if not balanced with other nutrients. The Mediterranean diet is also higher in monounsaturated fats and lowers in polyunsaturated fats than the DASH diet. These differences may account for some of the different effects these diets have on health. Overall, the DASH diet is a good way to eat for people who are looking to improve their health. It is low in sugar and high in fruits, vegetables, whole grains, and low-fat dairy products. The Mediterranean diet is also a good way to eat, but it may be more balanced for people who are looking to maintain their weight.

5.2 The Paleo Diet vs. the Mediterranean Diet

The Mediterranean diet is one of the most popular diets in the world, and for a good reason. It is packed with nutrients and antioxidants, and it has been shown to protect against diseases like heart disease, stroke, and cancer. Here is a look at the main difference and similarities between the Paleo diet and the Mediterranean diet.

The Paleo diet is based on the theory that humans were originally hunter-gatherers who ate a diet consisting mainly of meat, nuts, and vegetables. The Paleo diet is not recommended for people who are pregnant or breastfeeding, as it can be harmful to their health.

The Mediterranean diet is based on the theory that humans were originally farmers who ate a diet consisting of grains, fruits, and vegetables. The Mediterranean diet is generally recommended for people who are pregnant or breastfeeding, as it can be beneficial to their health. However, some variations of the Mediterranean diet include moderate amounts of meat.

Both the Paleo diet and the Mediterranean diet are considered healthy diets. They both contain nutrients and antioxidants that can protect against diseases. The key difference between the two diets is that the Paleo diet is not recommended for pregnant or breastfeeding women, while the Mediterranean diet is generally safe for these groups of people.

5.3 The Average American Diet vs. the Mediterranean Diet

The ordinary American diet (or the diet of the average individual like you and me) is plainly a Mediterranean lifestyle. It does not involve a deliberate attempt to achieve specific results. That said, it is the polar opposite of the Mediterranean diet.

It is primarily characterized by the use of processed foods, refined carbs, fried foods, red meat, refined sugar, and high-fat dairy products. This type of diet is high in heart-harming trans fats and salt. Not only that, but To round out the bleak image, this diet is devoid of whole grains, fruits, and vegetables. This diet may be beneficial to the multibillion-dollar food and beverage business, but it is detrimental to the health and longevity of the hundreds of millions of Americans who consume it.

Those who consume what is plainly the dangerous typical American diet have a considerably more sedentary lifestyle, thanks to the love affair most Americans have with their cars, in contrast to the Southern Mediterranean people who supplement their healthy food with an active lifestyle. Though comparisons are always distasteful, comparing the Mediterranean Diet to the disease-inducing average American diet is hardly worth the work.

5.4 The Atkins Diet vs. the Mediterranean Diet

One popular variation of the Mediterranean diet is the Atkins diet. The Atkins diet is a low-carbohydrate, high-fat diet. It is similar to the Mediterranean diet in that it is low in saturated fat, cholesterol, and sugar. However, the Atkins diet includes more processed foods than the Mediterranean diet. The two diets also have different amounts of protein. The Atkins diet recommends that 20 to 30 percent of your daily caloric intake come from protein, while the Mediterranean diet recommends about 10 to 15 percent of your daily caloric intake come from protein. The two diets also have different amounts of carbohydrates. The Atkins diet allows up to 50 grams of carbohydrates per day, while the Mediterranean diet allows up to 60 grams of carbohydrates per day. The two diets have several other differences. The Atkins diet is more restrictive in terms of what types of foods you can eat, while the Mediterranean diet allows for more variety. The Atkins diet also recommends avoiding saturated fats, while the Mediterranean diet allows for a moderate amount of saturated fat. The two diets also have different recommendations for how often you should exercise. The Atkins diet recommends doing moderate amounts of exercise every day, while the Mediterranean diet does not recommend any specific amount of exercise.

6 FOOD CONSUMPTION GUIDELINES

The first thing that you will want to look at when it comes to starting on a new diet plan is the foods that you are allowed to consume on this diet plan. With this diet plan, it is important that you spend your time eating foods that are wholesome and full of nutrients. If you are able to find foods that only have one ingredient in them, then you are well on your way to getting all of the good health benefits that you are looking for.

There are a lot of great meals that you will be able to eat on this diet plan. You are going to love all of the great flavor and more that you can get, especially considering there will be no added sugars or preservatives in this meal plan. It is all-natural and wholesome, and you are going to feel so much better in a short amount of time.

Some of the foods that you are able to eat when you choose to go on this kind of diet plan include:

6.1 Foods To Consume Plenty

6.1.1 Fish and Seafood

The Mediterranean diet is known for its high intake of fish and seafood. These foods are considered to be healthy because they are high in unsaturated fats and antioxidants. Some fish to consider include:

- Salmon: This fish is high in omega-3 fatty acids and is a great source of protein. It can be cooked in many ways, including grilled or baked.
- Shrimp: These small shrimps are packed with protein and vitamins, and minerals. They can be cooked in many ways, including stir-fry or grilled.
- Mussels: Mussels are a popular seafood choice in the Mediterranean diet. They are high in zinc and have low levels of cholesterol. They can be steamed or boiled.
- Tilapia: Tilapia is a healthy fish that is low in fat and cholesterol. It can be grilled, baked, or broiled.
- Sardines: Sardines are another good fish choice for the Mediterranean diet. They are high in EPA and DHA fatty acids, which are beneficial for your health. Sardines can be grilled, boiled, or fried.

6.1.2 Vegetables and Fruits

A Mediterranean diet is healthy because it emphasizes the consumption of fruits and vegetables. These foods are packed with vitamins, minerals, antioxidants, and fiber. They are also low in saturated fat and cholesterol.

One of the best ways to enjoy a Mediterranean diet is to fill up on fruits and vegetables every day. Here are some of the most common vegetables and fruits that are featured in this type of diet:

Vegetables:

- Artichokes
- Asparagus
- Beans
- Bell Peppers
- Broccoli
- Celery
- Cucumbers
- Eggplant
- Fennel bulb
- Garlic
- Green beans
- Lettuce (e.g. romaine, garden, Boston)
- Mushrooms (e.g. shiitake, portobello)
- Okra
- Onion
- Parsley
- Peppers (e.g. bell, jalapeño, anaheim)
- Potatoes

- Rutabaga
- Spinach
- Tomatoes

Fruits:

- Avocados
- Bananas
- Cherries
- Dates
- Figs
- Grapefruit
- Kiwifruit
- Lemons
- Mandarin oranges
- Mango
- Melons (e.g. honeydew, watermelon)
- Orange juice
- Papaya
- Pineapple
- Plums
- Pomegranate juice
- Raspberries
- Strawberries
- Tangerines

6.1.3 Nuts and Seeds

If you're following a Mediterranean diet, you might want to add some nuts to your daily routine. Nuts are a great source of healthy fats and antioxidants, which can protect you against diseases. In fact, a study published in the journal "Nutrition Research" found that people who ate more nuts had a lower risk of developing heart disease, cancer, and Alzheimer's disease. Here are six nuts that are especially beneficial to a Mediterranean diet:

1. Walnuts

Walnuts are an excellent source of omega-3 fatty acids, which can help protect your heart health. They also contain vitamin E, magnesium, and zinc.

2. Pecans

Pecans are another great option for those following a Mediterranean diet. They're high in fiber and contain antioxidants like beta-carotene and selenium. Additionally, they're loaded with monounsaturated fats and minerals like copper and iron.

3. Cashews

Cashews are a good source of both Omega-6 and Omega-3 fatty acids. They also contain vitamins B6 and E, which can support cognitive function and reduce the risk of heart disease.

4. Almonds

Almonds area good source of both Omega-6 and Omega-3 fatty acids. They also contain fiber, magnesium, and copper.

5. Brazil Nuts

Brazil nuts are a great source of selenium, a mineral that is important for thyroid health and the prevention of cancer.

6. Macadamia Nuts

Macadamia nuts are high in antioxidants and monounsaturated fats, which can help reduce the risk of heart disease and promote healthy skin.

6.1.4 Legumes

Legumes are another food group that you can focus on as well. You can choose from some different options to add to your meals, including chickpeas, peanuts, lentils, peas, and beans.

6.1.5 Whole Grains And Potatoes

You can eat some fantastic whole grains, but make sure you choose whole grain pasta and bread rather than white pasta and bread loaded with sugars and other processed ingredients. When you're trying to load up your plate, these can assist quite a deal.

There are numerous whole grain options to include in your meals, and the recipes in this manual will help you incorporate as many as you need. Whole oats, buckwheat, couscous, barley, rye, brown rice, whole wheat pasta, whole wheat bread, sweet potatoes, turnips, and white potatoes are some of the alternatives.

Keep in mind that you can eat as much whole grain bread and pasta as you like with this group. However, you should avoid any white kinds of pasta and bread that are deemed processed. These will not give you the same vitamins and nutrients as whole grains will, and they should be avoided as much as possible.

6.1.6 Herbs and Spices

In a Mediterranean diet, herbs and spices are a big part of the cuisine. There are many different types of herbs and spices that can be used in cooking, and each has its own unique flavor and aroma. Here are some of the most common herbs and spices used in Mediterranean cuisine:

- Basil: Basil is a popular herb in Mediterranean cuisine. It has a strong minty flavor and is often used in Greek salads or as a garnish on dishes.
- Cinnamon: Cinnamon is another common herb used in Mediterranean cuisine. It has a warm, spicy flavor that can add depth to dishes.
- Cilantro: Cilantro is a popular herb found in Mexican, South American, and some Mediterranean dishes. It has a delicate, lemony flavor that pairs well with other spices.
- Garlic: Garlic is one of the key ingredients in many Mediterranean recipes. Its strong garlic flavor makes it an essential component of many dishes.
- Oregano: Oregano is another common herb found in Mediterranean cuisine. Its strong herbal flavor can be seen in dishes like Greek hummus or Italian pesto sauce.
- Sage: Sage is a common herb used in Mediterranean cuisine. Its flavor is reminiscent of woodsy notes, and it can be used in dishes like lamb or chicken dishes.
- Tarragon: Tarragon is another common herb used in Mediterranean cuisine. Its flavor is reminiscent of licorice, and it can be used in dishes like chicken or fish dishes.
- Thyme: Thyme is another common herb used in Mediterranean cuisine. Its flavor is reminiscent of a bouquet of flowers, and it can be used in dishes like vegetable or fish dishes.
- Za'atar: Za'atar is a common herb found in Mediterranean cuisine. Its flavor is reminiscent of French lavender, and it can be used in dishes like lamb or chicken dishes.

Other common ingredients in Mediterranean cuisine include olives, lemon, feta cheese, and balsamic vinegar.

6.1.7 Healthy Fats

One of the most important aspects of adopting the Mediterranean diet is eating plenty of healthy fats. These will help you stay full and fed for extended periods of time, allowing you to consume fewer calories overall.

When it comes to finding the good fats that will benefit you on this diet plan, you have a few different possibilities. When it comes to healthy fats, extra virgin olive oil reigns supreme on this diet. However, there are additional healthy fats to consider, such as coconut oil, avocado oil, avocados, and olives.

6.2 Foods That You Can Have in Moderation

With the list of foods above, you can eat as many of those as you would like. As long as you learn how to listen to your body and only eat until you are hungry, you will find that you can enjoy as many of those foods as you want. But there are some other foods that you need to enjoy more in moderation on this diet plan. They aren't taken out of the diet, but you shouldn't consume them as much as you do some of the other foods above. Some of the foods that you should eat in moderation include:

Read Meat

Too much red meat can increase your risk of heart disease and other health problems, so it's important to choose the right types of red meat when following this diet.

Ideally, you should limit yourself to no more than two servings per week of red meat, which includes lamb, beef, pork, and veal. If you do choose to include red meat in your diet, make sure to select leaner cuts that have less fat and cholesterol. Try to avoid high-fat meats like bacon and sausage, which are packed with calories and harmful fats.

Dairy

Some dairy products that are generally consumed on the Mediterranean diet are cheese, yogurt, milk, and eggs. These foods can provide a good amount of calcium and other nutrients that are essential for healthy bones and teeth. However, if you are following the Mediterranean diet in moderation, you should avoid dairy products that contain high levels of saturated fat or cholesterol.

Eggs

As long as you eat them in moderation, eggs are just fine on this diet plan. They are going to provide you with a good amount of protein and can be a great way to start out the morning. And you can cook them in any manner that you would like, such as hard-boiled, fried, poached, or scrambled.

Poultry

Poultry can be another great way for you to get in the protein that you are looking for to keep your body healthy. But you do need to eat it in moderation, rather than all of the time. One option would be turkey, which can help you to get lots of good protein and other nutrients as well.

6.3 Foods To Avoid While Following A Mediterranean Diet

When following the Mediterranean diet, it's important to keep your diet balanced and include a variety of foods. While there are many healthy options to choose from, you should avoid certain types of food when following this diet.

Below are a few foods to avoid when following the Mediterranean diet:

- Processed foods: These foods typically contain high levels of sugar, salt, and unhealthy fats. Instead of eating these types of foods on a regular basis, make sure to eat them in moderation whenever possible.
- Chips and other unhealthy snacks: Snacks such as chips and candy are typically high in calories and unhealthy fats. Instead of eating these types of snacks, try enjoying a small piece of fruit or yogurt instead.
- Deep-fried items: Many items at fast food restaurants or convenience stores are deep-fried. These foods are not only unhealthy but also often contain high amounts of saturated fat. Instead of eating these types of foods, try opting for healthier snacks such as salad or fruit.
- Alcohol: While alcoholic beverages are not typically considered part of the Mediterranean diet, they can still be unhealthy if consumed in large amounts. Limit yourself to one or two drinks per day, and make sure to avoid sugary drinks as well.

By following these guidelines, you can maintain a healthy Mediterranean diet while still enjoying delicious food.

6.4 Oils to know about

One of the best ways to implement a Mediterranean-style diet is to use oils. Many of these oils are beneficial for your health and can be used in many different ways. Here are a few of the best oils to use on a Mediterranean diet:

- Extra-virgin olive oil is a great option for cooking and can be used in salad dressing, dips, pasta sauces, and even as a main dish. It's packed with antioxidants and has been linked with lower rates of heart disease, obesity, and cancer.
- Canola oil is another good option for cooking. It's low in saturated fat and has been shown to be helpful in reducing inflammation and controlling blood sugar levels.
- Sesame oil is known for its anti-inflammatory properties and can be used in many different ways, including as a dipping sauce or as part of a stir-fry.
- Flaxseed oil is high in omega-3 fatty acids, which have been linked with a number of health benefits, such as reducing the risk of heart disease, lowering cholesterol levels, boosting brain function, and improving joint health.
- Cold-pressed sesame oil is a great option for those who are looking for a healthier version of soy sauce. It's low in calories and has a mild flavor that can be used in many different dishes.
- Coconut oil is a great option for baking and can be used in place of vegetable oil or butter. It's high in saturated fat but has a low-calorie count, making it a great choice for those looking to cut down on their overall caloric intake.
- Ghee is a type of clarified butter that is made from milk and has a high-fat content. It's been shown to be beneficial for cholesterol levels and can be used in place of other types of fats in recipes.

7 HOW THE DIET CAN HELP WITH WEIGHT LOSS

Mediterranean diets are known for being high in fiber, healthy fats, and antioxidants. These diets have been shown to be effective for weight loss because they help control cravings and provide a variety of nutrients that help maintain energy levels. They also promote a healthy weight distribution and can help prevent heart disease, cancer, and other chronic illnesses.

That is the beauty of working with this diet plan. It isn't just something that you lose weight on quickly and then gains it all back. Instead, it is a series of healthy lifestyle choices that will all come together to help you to lose weight. And it all happens by eating foods that are delicious and have a lot of flavors while enjoying life. It is so much better than wasting your time and stressing out about counting calories all the time.

7.1 Focusing On The Mediterranean Dietary Style

The main thing that is different about this diet plan compared to some of the others that you may have heard about in the past is that it is not just about the foods you eat; it is about making healthy changes to every part of your life. You need to take some time to pay attention to lifestyle changes, including exercising more often, changing your portion sizes, socializing, and drinking more water, in order to see the long-term results. There are a lot of diets for weight loss out there, but many of them are going to come and go. They may help you lose weight, but the weight loss may be short-term, or the diet plan is too difficult to stick with.

This isn't what you will see with the Mediterranean diet. With this choice, you will start to pay more attention to your individual lifestyle, including your stress levels, your socialization, the types of foods that you decide to eat, how much physical activity you add to your life, your portion sizes, and more. You can start to change these things each day, and then this forces you into some great long-term habits that will help you to lose weight and keep it off.

- Eat More Fruits and Vegetables: The mainstay of the Mediterranean diet is fruits and vegetables, both of which are high in antioxidants and other nutrients that help promote weight loss. Aim to eat at least five servings of fruits and vegetables per day.
- Choose Leaner Meat Options: Just because the Mediterranean diet is high in healthy foods doesn't mean you have to give up your favorite meat dishes. In fact, choosing leaner meats can help you lose weight while eating in accordance with the Mediterranean diet guidelines. Try opting for chicken instead of beef or lamb or using skinless poultry instead of fatty poultry like chicken thighs or drumsticks.
- Avoid Processed Foods: Many processed foods are loaded with sugar, sodium, and unhealthy fats. Limit your intake of processed foods to a few times per week.
- Drink Plenty of Water: A lack of water can lead to weight gain because it causes the body to retain water weight. Aim to drink at least 8 cups of water per day.
- Exercise Regularly: According to the National Institutes of Health, regular exercise can help you lose weight and improve your overall health. Workout for 30 minutes on most days of the week.

7.2 How to Pay Attention to Calories Without Counting Them

Even on the Mediterranean diet, you need to be careful with the number of calories that you consume. But you don't need to spend your time counting those calories. These calories are going to be a big concept when it comes to losing weight. Basically, the calories are going to be the amount of energy that

is found in the foods you eat, as well as the amount of energy that your body is going to use as you move through the day.
Your body is always in need of fuel or energy, not only for daily activities like exercising, cleaning, cooking, and more, but also for the basic biological functions that you do, such as thinking and breathing. Everyone is going to have a different metabolism. And your own personal metabolic rate is going to determine how fast you are able to burn calories. This can depend on your physical fitness level, genetics, gender, and age.
No matter what, though, you will not be able to lose weight if you take in more calories than you are able to burn through daily activity and exercise. If you want to be able to lose weight, you need to be able to create a calorie deficit, but you can do this without having to actually count out all of the calories that you eat and all that you burn. Making some small changes to your lifestyle, like exercising more and reducing how big your portions are, can help you to reduce the number of calories that you take in.

7.3 How to Suppress Your Appetite

One of the biggest issues that a lot of people face when they go on a diet plan is that they feel hungry. Their bodies are used to eating a ton of food, and not being able to eat as much can make them feel off. The good news is that when you follow the Mediterranean diet the proper way, you will be able to eat lots of healthy foods that will keep your appetite to a minimum, even if you are eating fewer calories than before. If you're looking to lose weight on the Mediterranean diet, you need to be mindful of how much food you're eating. The Mediterranean diet is known for its high-quality, plant-based foods and moderate amounts of dairy. However, if you're looking to lose weight on the Mediterranean diet, you might be tempted to overeat. Here are some tips on how to suppress your appetite in a healthy way:

- Eat slowly and chew your food well.
- Drink plenty of water and avoid sugary beverages.
- Enjoy your food but don't overeat.
- Avoid eating late at night or in front of the TV.
- Practice portion control and eat smaller meals throughout the day

7.4 Lead A Stress-Free Life

Stress can cause a lot of hormones to go everywhere. And when we are in the fight or flight response of our stress hormones, it is really hard to make good nutritional decisions that are going to help us lose weight, as well as improve other aspects of our health. Because of this, it is so important that you learn how to reduce your stress. You need to be the one in control over your diet and the things that you do in life, not your hormones. And reducing stress can make that so much easier.
There are a lot of things that you can do to reduce stress, and as long as they aren't something unhealthy like drinking heavily or smoking, then you can choose the one that is right for you. Pick something that allows you to take care of yourself. Choose something that is easy to stick with. Do something that is just for yourself and has nothing to do with all of your obligations. Whether it is reading a book for a few minutes, devotionals, spending time with some friends, taking a bath, or something else, try to carve out a few minutes a day when you can put things aside and just focus on what you want to.
As you can see, there are a lot of reasons why you would want to use the Mediterranean diet to help you to lose weight. If you are like many Americans, or even many people throughout the world, trying to stay healthy and lose weight can be hard. But when you are following this kind of diet plan, you will be

able to keep your hormones in check, reduce stress, and eat lots of healthy foods while being more active. When all of this comes together, weight loss will be a breeze.

7.5 Reasons Why You May "Not" Be Losing Weight

Are you not seeing the results you want with your diet? One big reason why people may not be losing weight on a Mediterranean diet is that they are not properly digesting the food.

The Mediterranean diet is rich in fiber, which can help to keep you full and prevent overeating. If you are not digesting your food properly, your body will not be able to extract all of the nutrients that it needs. This can lead to weight gain and other health problems. Make sure that you are eating enough fiber each day by including plenty of fruits, vegetables, and whole grains in your diet.

Are you not meeting your daily calorie goals? If you are not consuming enough calories, your body will start to burn muscle instead of fat. This can lead to weight loss stalls and even weight gain in some cases. Make sure that you are keeping track of how many calories you are eating each day, and make sure that you are adding in enough protein and healthy fats to balance out your caloric intake.

Are you lacking in essential vitamins and minerals? One of the benefits of a Mediterranean diet is that it is rich in antioxidants and other nutrients that help to support weight loss. Make sure that you include plenty of fruits, vegetables, nuts, and whole grains in your diet to get the nutrients that you need to lose weight.

Do you have any food allergies or intolerances? If you have any allergies or intolerances, it can be difficult to tolerate specific foods in a Mediterranean diet. This can lead to difficulty losing weight and other health problems. If you think that you may have a food allergy or intolerance, talk to your doctor about testing for these conditions.

8 COMMON MISTAKES TO AVOID

When starting anything new, mistakes are unavoidable. In this chapter, I am going to give you a quick rundown of some of the mistakes I made when I first started eating the Mediterranean way, as well as share some slipups friends and family members had.

8.1 Keeping Your Portions In Check

I know I've been going on and on about moderation. I will, unfortunately, have to talk about it some more under the guise of portion control. Managing how much you eat is particularly important if you're trying to lose weight, but it is also a factor if you want to maintain your weight and, with it, your health. Portion control is important for staying healthy because it can help you maintain a healthy weight, control your calorie intake, and avoid overeating. It's also important to remember that not all calories are created equal. Some calories are more filling than others, so it's important to eat enough of the right kinds of foods to stay on track.

8.2 Overloading On Carbs

The Mediterranean diet is high in fiber and low in processed foods, which can make it a great choice for people who are looking to drop weight. However, if you're not careful with how much carbohydrates you eat, you could end up overloading on carbs and putting your health at risk. The key to avoiding this problem is to divide your carbohydrates into smaller servings throughout the day rather than eating large amounts all at once. This way, you'll stay satisfied and won't be tempted to overeat later on.

8.3 Not Eating Enough Fish

You won't reap the heart- and brain-boosting health benefits of fish and seafood if you don't eat enough of it. Aim for three times a week, and you'll get all the omega-3 fatty acids your brain and body need. If you're a vegetarian or you dislike seafood, don't worry, just supplement with fish and seaweed oil.

8.4 Eating the Wrong Dairy

Dairy is a mainstay of many Mediterranean diets, but it's important to be aware of the types of dairy that are best suited for this diet. Some popular dairy products that are typically not recommended for the Mediterranean diet include full-fat dairy products and processed foods with added sugar. Instead, opt for low-fat or non-dairy versions of these products when possible. Additionally, limit your intake of milk and other dairy products during the day to two cups per day. This will help to keep your blood sugar levels stable and give you the nutrients you need to maintain a healthy weight.

8.5 Not Having Enough Beans

Beans should be part of the healthy foundation of the Mediterranean meal plan. Some people prefer to leave this superfood off their plates because it takes longer to prepare than other food, and beans give some people gas. Beans are a great source of protein, fiber, and B vitamins, which are all important for a healthy diet. They also contain anti-inflammatory properties, which can help reduce the risk of diseases such as cancer.

8.6 Thinking Wine is Water

One of the most common mistakes people make when following a Mediterranean diet is drinking too much wine. While wine is a welcome part of many Mediterranean-style dishes, overindulging can lead to weight gain and other health problems. Moderation is key when it comes to wine consumption, so aim for no more than two glasses per day.

8.7 Using Extra-Virgin Olive Oil at a High Heat

It can be tempting to use extra virgin olive oil at high heat when cooking Mediterranean-style dishes, but this can lead to problems. Extra virgin olive oil is a delicate oil and can easily break down or scorch if used too quickly or at high heat. In fact, the FDA recommends using it only at low or medium heat.

8.8 Not Following The 10 Commandments

It's not as serious as it sounds, I promise. The 10 commandments perfectly sum up what the Mediterranean Diet and lifestyle are all about. And, if you follow them diligently, you're set to gain a healthy body and a longer life.

Don't worry if you wander off the path now and again. You won't be condemned to a sickly life spent in an out-of-shape body. Just get back to following the Mediterranean Diet and living the lifestyle, and you'll be a-okay.

The ten commandments of the Mediterranean Diet and lifestyle are:

- Fill your plate with an abundance of fresh, non-processed food.
- Do not let any saturated fat, trans fat, sodium, or refined sugar cross your lips.
- Don't use margarine or butter; in its place, use olive oil or trans- fat-free vegetable spread.
- Eat your fill of vegetables but limit the portions of other foods.
- Drink enough water.

- Don't drink too much red wine.
- Get your heart rate up for at least 30 minutes a day.
- Don't smoke.
- Unwind and relax, specifically after eating.
- Laugh a lot, smile, and enjoy life.

9 WEEK-ROUND SHOPPING LIST

Shopping list items vary from country to country, and also items change according to seasons. Your first choice should be seasonal and local ingredients. No need to buy fancy and expensive imported ingredients. Here is a basic list mentioned below:

Vegetables:

- Zucchini
- Tomatoes
- Spinach
- Potatoes
- Peppers
- Peas
- Onion
- Okra
- Mushrooms
- Green beans
- Garlic
- Eggplant
- Cucumber
- Celery
- Cauliflower
- Carrots
- Cabbage
- Broccoli
- Beets

Greens:

- Chicory
- Dandelions
- Beet greens
- Amaranth

Fruits:

- Orange
- Lemons
- Apples
- Pears
- Cherries
- Watermelon
- Cantaloupe
- Peaches
- Pears
- Figs
- Apricots

Dairy Products:

- Plain Greek yogurt
- Sheep's milk yogurt
- Feta cheese
- Fresh cheese like ricotta
- Parmesan
- Mozzarella
- Graviera
- Mizithra

Meat And Poultry:

They should be eaten rarely, like once a week.

- Chicken
- Beef
- Veal
- Pork

Fish and Seafood:

Preferably eat small fatty fish. You can eat canned fish as well.

- Anchovies
- Sardines

- Shrimp
- Calamari
- Herbs Snd Spices:
- Oregano
- Parsley
- Dill

Grains and Bread:

- Mint
- Basil
- Whole grain bread
- Whole grain breadsticks
- Pita bread
- Cumin
- Allspice
- Cinnamon
- Phyllo
- Pasta
- Rice
- Bulgur
- Pepper
- Sea salt
- Sage
- Couscous

Fats and Nuts:

- Extra virgin olive oil
- Tahini
- Almonds
- Walnuts
- Pine nuts
- Pistachios
- Sesame seeds
- Beans:
- Lentils
- Chickpeas
- White Beans
- Fava Beans
- Pantry Items:
- Canned tomatoes
- Olives
- Sun-dried tomatoes
- Capers
- Honey
- Thyme
- Herbal Tea

10 A NOTE ON MEAL PREP

Meal prep is the process of preparing meals ahead of time so that you can have them on hand when you need them. It can be a great way to save time and money, and it can also be a healthy way to eat. There are many different types of meal prep, and it can be done with or without food storage.

10.1 Exploring The Concept Of Meal Prepping

Prepping meals can be a lot of work, but it's worth it to have healthy, well-balanced meals that are easy to grab and go. There are a lot of different ways to prep meals, but one popular way is to meal prep in bulk. This means cooking a bunch of different meals and storing them in containers so you can easily grab one and go. Keeping that in mind, let us dissect Meal Prepping a bit more.

"Meal Prepping is the process of planning what you are going to eat (and how you are going to make it) ahead of time."

The core objective of prepping your meal ahead of time is to:

- Help you save a lot in the money-saving department by allowing you to set up a rough estimate of your food budget early on ahead.
- Enforce you to stick to the plan and eat as much healthy food as possible.
- Minimize food wastage.
- Clear your head off the burden of "What to cook next" and ease your mind by minimizing any food-related stress.
- Prevent the wasting of time by letting you know exactly "What" you are going to eat and "When."

- Help you avoid monotony in your daily meal by spicing up the routine from time to time.

10.2 Amazing Advantages Of Meal Prep

- It helps you to save a lot of money by allowing you to set up a rough estimate of your food budget ahead of time
- It allows you to stick to a healthy plan and eat as much healthy food as possible
- It minimizes food wastage
- It clears off the burden of "What you should cook next" and eases your mind, clearing it up of any food-related stress.
- Prevent the wasting of time by letting you know exactly "What" you are going to eat and "When."
- Help you avoid monotony in your daily meal by spicing up the routine from time to time.
- Meal Prepping helps you to control your portions by adjusting a set amount of food per meal. This gives you greater control over what you eat, helping in weight loss as well
- Greater control of your food routine will help you create a more balanced and nutritious diet plan in the long run
- Since everything is pre-planned, it will help you to avoid the rush of "Last minute preparations" and make the cooking process more comfortable for you
- Meal Prepping will help you to seamlessly multitask with other famous works, as opposed to sitting in the kitchen all day to cook. Since you will keep everything prepared, it will save a lot of time from your daily routine and allow you to focus on other activities.

10.3 The Ideas to Know About

Keep in mind that the following are just some of the hundreds of Meal Prep ideas that are designed to inspire you to explore and come up with your own ideas as well!

Use the following as references as to how you can prepare the ingredients and store them prior to cooking.

Make A Plan Ahead Of Time: If you are reading this book, then you have probably decided to go on a Clean Eating diet journey. An excellent way to start this off is to start with a small number of recipes, for perhaps 7 days. Choose which recipes you are going to use and make a rough idea inside your head. Make a list and buy the ingredients accordingly ahead of time.

Keep A Good Supply Of Mason Jars: Mason jars are terrific, not only for storing memories! But also for storing healthy salads! Assuming that you are a good buff, it might be a good idea to prepare your salads ahead of time and store them in mason jars. Make sure to keep the salad dressing at the bottom of the jar to ensure that nothing greens don't get soggy!

Three-Way Seasoning In One Pan: If your diet requires you to stick with lean meats such as chicken, then seasoning them from time to time might become somewhat of a chore. A simple solution to that is to prepare a pan with aluminum foil dividers. Using these will allow you to season three or more (depending on how many dividers you are using) types of chicken seasoning to be done using the same pan!

Boil Eggs In An Oven Instead Of A Pot: Now, this might sound a little bit weird at first, but it is highly effective! The problem here comes with the number of eggs that can be boiled in one go. If you are using a standard-sized pot, then you would probably be able to squeeze in 5 or 6 eggs max in one batch. However, if you try to bake your eggs in muffin tins using an oven, then you will be able to get a dozen or perfectly hard-boiled eggs in no time!

Keep Your Prepared Smoothies Frozen In Muffin Tins: Plopping out some different ingredients early in the morning might be a chore for some people. A simple solution to that is to go ahead and freeze up your blended smoothies in muffin tins. This will not only save up time but will also give you a good dose of satisfaction as you wake up in the morning and toss a few "smoothie cups" into the blender for a simple yet healthy breakfast.

Roast Vegetables That Require The Same Time In One Batch: When you are preparing large batches of vegetables for roasting, it is smart to go ahead and create batches of vegetables depending on how long they take to roast. For example, you can create a batch of rapid-cooking vegetables such as mushrooms, asparagus, or cherry tomatoes and a batch of slow-roasting veggies such as potatoes, cauliflowers, and carrots to minimize time loss and maximize output.

Learn To Effectively Use A Skewer: When you think of skewers, you automatically think of kabobs! But Skewers aren't necessarily designed to be used only with street meats. Wooden skewers can help you to measure how much meat you are going to consume in one go. So, you can punch in your meat in multiple skewers and divide them evenly and store them for the rest of the week. When the time comes, take out one skewer and cook it up!

Keep A Good Supply Of Sectioned Plastic Containers: Sectioned containers like the one shown above are an absolute necessity for serious meal-prepping savants! These will effortlessly give you enough space to separate every single component of your meal while making sure that you don't mix everything up and create a mess. The separate ingredients would also be straightforward to find and use!

Keep A Tab Of Your Accomplishments: This is perhaps the essential aspect of a meal prepping routine. Always make sure to measure your progress somehow and set small milestones for you to accomplish. Achieving these milestones will encourage you and inspire you further to keep pushing yourself until you reach your final goal. Alternatively, looking at your positive progress will significantly motivate you to push forward as well. Now that you have a basic understanding of the concepts of diet and meal prepping let me give you a breakdown of just some of the fantastic benefits of meal prep!

Different Types Of I hope that meal prep will become a regular routine in your home like it is in ours. In order to make that happen, it is essential that you invest in and choose the right storage containers. When I was ready to invest in a set of containers, I bought a few different options—glass, metal, and plastic (BPA-free, of course). This way, I could do a trial run to figure out what I liked best before I made a big purchase. Trying a few to see what you like and what works best in your kitchen will save you time and money in the long run.

Good-quality containers are essential for keeping your food fresh as long as possible. Here are some things to look for when buying containers for meal prepping:

BPA-free.

If you're looking for a safe and environmentally friendly way to store your belongings, you may want to consider using storage containers made of plastic that are free of bisphenol A (BPA). BPA is a chemical that is often used in the manufacturing of plastics, and it has been linked to health concerns such as hormone disruption and developmental issues in children.

There are a variety of storage containers made without BPA, and some of the most popular options include glass and stainless steel containers. While there are some benefits to using these types of containers, they may not be ideal for all situations. For example, glass containers are heavier than plastic ones, which can make them more difficult to move around. Additionally, stainless steel containers can be difficult to clean if they get dirty.

If you're undecided about which type of storage container is best for you, it's worth considering your needs and preferences before making a decision. There are plenty of options available that will meet your needs without exposing you or your belongings to dangerous chemicals.

Stackable.

I know we all have a cupboard or a drawer packed full of containers and lids. If you begin to make meal prep a part of your regular routine, that means a lot of containers will start to accumulate. Having containers that are stackable will keep your cupboards functional and looking organized, making life easier.

Freezer-safe.

A freezer-safe container is a great option for long-term storage because it's temperature and humidity resistant. This type of container is also ideal for storing perishable items, like food. These containers are made of heavy-duty materials, like steel, and can hold a lot of weight. They're also easy to clean.

Microwave-safe.

Another type of microwave-safe food storage container is the Pyrex container. Pyrex is a popular brand name for glassware that is heat resistant up to 480 °F. Pyrex containers are often used to store foods like soups, stews, and chili in the oven or microwave.

In addition to storing food in traditional storage containers, there are also special holders designed specifically for microwave use. These holders are often called "microwave mugs" or "microwave pouches," and they come in different sizes and shapes to fit any type of food.

Dishwasher-safe.

Dishwasher-safe containers are designed to be washed in a dishwasher. This means that they will not corrode or warp over time, making them ideal for storing food. Non-dishwasher-safe containers, on the other hand, may not be able to be washed in a dishwasher, but they are still generally safe to use. They may have a coating that makes them resistant to moisture and corrosion, or they may simply be made from thicker materials that are more durable.

If you need to store food in a container that will not be washed in a dishwasher, it is important to choose a container that is made from a non-corroding material. Some examples of non-corroding materials include glass or stainless steel. If you need to store food in a container that will be washed in a dishwasher, it is best to choose a container that is made from plastic or silicone.

Glass Containers

Glass containers are one type of storage container that is becoming increasingly popular. Here are some reasons why glass containers are a good choice for storage:

- They are lightweight and easy to move around.
- They are shatterproof and unbreakable.
- They can be recycled.

If you're looking for a storage container that is environmentally friendly and will last for years, glass is a great option.

Plastic Containers

Plastic containers are very popular for meal prep— they're lightweight, stack easily, and many are now micro-waivable as well as freezable. But as I mentioned, my go-to is glass. Plastic containers may leach harmful substances into the food stored in them. Plastic is not biodegradable, which means it isn't possible for our earth to naturally absorb the material back into the soil; instead, plastic actually contaminates it. Unlike glass and metal, plastic absorbs odors and tastes like whatever you stored in it previously. If you have ever stored fish in a plastic container, I'm guessing it still smells like fish to this day. While it's a fact that plastic is cheaper than other options, it's also true that it will not last as long. If you do choose to go with plastic containers, always look for an indicator that they are BPA-free.

Mason Jars

Mason (canning) jars are also great for storing food. Mason jars, which are made of glass, are inexpensive and ideal for storing salads and salad dressings. A combination of wide- mouth quart and pint jars, as well as some smaller four- ounce jars for dressings, will go a long way when doing meal preps. I incorporate them a few times throughout the preps for quick storage.

Stainless Steel

Stainless steel food containers are ideal for storing and transporting food. They are durable, leakproof, and easy to clean. They come in a variety of sizes and shapes, so you can find the perfect one for your needs. Here are some of the most common types of stainless steel food containers:

1. Food storage container sets. These sets come with a variety of different-sized containers, so you can easily store your food in one place.
2. Glass storage jars. These jars are perfect for storing small amounts of food. They are also easy to clean and sterilize.
3. Plastic storage containers. These containers are perfect for storing large quantities of food. They are durable, and they don't corrode or rust over time.
4. Stainless steel pots and pans. Stainless steel pots and pans are ideal for cooking and baking foods. They are resistant to heat, so they won't damage your food or cookware.
5. Stainless steel bowls and plates. These bowls and plates are perfect for serving food to customers or guests. They are dishwasher-safe, so you can easily clean them afterward.

10.4 Different Types Of Storage

I hope meal prep will become a regular routine in your home like ours. To make that happen, you must invest in and choose the right storage containers. When I was ready to invest in a set of containers, I bought a few different options—glass, metal, and plastic (BPA-free, of course). This way, I could do a trial run to determine what I liked best before making a big purchase. Trying a few to see what you like and what works best in your kitchen will save you time and money in the long run.

Good-quality containers are essential for keeping your food fresh as long as possible. Here are some things to look for when buying containers for meal prepping:

BPA-free.

Suppose you're looking for a safe and environmentally friendly way to store your belongings. In that case, you may consider using storage containers made of plastic free of bisphenol A (BPA). BPA is a chemical often used in manufacturing plastics, and it has been linked to health concerns such as hormone disruption and developmental issues in children.

There are a variety of storage containers made without BPA, and some of the most popular options include glass and stainless steel containers. While there are some benefits to using these containers, they may not be ideal for all situations. For example, glass containers are heavier than plastic ones, making them more difficult to move around. Additionally, stainless steel containers can be difficult to clean if they get dirty.

Suppose you're undecided about which type of storage container is best for you. In that case, it's worth considering your needs and preferences before deciding. Plenty of options will meet your needs without exposing you or your belongings to dangerous chemicals.

Stackable.

I know we all have a cupboard or a drawer packed full of containers and lids. If you begin to make meal prep a part of your regular routine, a lot of containers will start to accumulate. Stackable containers will keep your cupboards functional and organized, making life easier.

Freezer-safe.

A freezer-safe container is a great option for long-term storage because it's temperature and humidity resistant. This container is also ideal for storing perishable items, like food. These containers are heavy-duty materials, like steel, and can hold much weight. They're also easy to clean.

Microwave-safe.

Another type of microwave-safe food storage container is the Pyrex container. Pyrex is a popular brand name for glassware that is heat resistant up to 480 °F. Pyrex containers are often used to store foods like soups, stews, and chili in the oven or microwave.

In addition to storing food in traditional containers, there are special holders designed specifically for microwave use. These holders are often called "microwave mugs" or "microwave pouches," They come in different sizes and shapes to fit any type of food.

Dishwasher-safe.

Dishwasher-safe containers are designed to be washed in a dishwasher. This means they will not corrode or warp over time, making them ideal for storing food. Non-dishwasher-safe containers, on the other hand, may not be able to be washed in a dishwasher, but they are still generally safe to use. They may have a coating that makes them resistant to moisture and corrosion, or they may simply be made from thicker materials that are more durable.

Suppose you need to store food in a container that will not be washed in a dishwasher. In that case, choosing a container made from a non-corroding material is important. Some examples of non-corroding materials include glass or stainless steel. If you need to store food in a container that will be washed in a dishwasher, it is best to choose a container that is made from plastic or silicone.

Glass Containers

Glass containers are one type of storage container that is becoming increasingly popular. Here are some reasons why glass containers are a good choice for storage:

- They are lightweight and easy to move around.
- They are shatterproof and unbreakable.
- They can be recycled.

If you're looking for a storage container that is environmentally friendly and will last for years, glass is a great option.

Plastic Containers

Plastic containers are very popular for meal prep— they're lightweight, stack easily, and many are now micro- waivable and freezable. But as I mentioned, my go-to is glass. Plastic containers may leach harmful substances into the food stored in them. Plastic is not biodegradable, which means it isn't possible for our earth to naturally absorb the material back into the soil; instead, plastic actually contaminates it. Unlike glass and metal, plastic absorbs odors and tastes like whatever you stored in it previously. If you have ever stored fish in a plastic container, I'm guessing it still smells like fish to this day. While it's a fact that plastic is cheaper than other options, it's also true that it will not last as long. If you choose to go with plastic containers, always look for an indicator that they are BPA-free.

Mason Jars

Mason (canning) jars are also great for storing food. Made of glass, Mason jars are inexpensive and perfect for storing salads and salad dressings. A combination of wide-mouth quart and pint jars and some smaller four-ounce jars for dressings will go a long way when preparing meals. I incorporate them a few times throughout the preps for quick storage.

Stainless Steel

Stainless steel food containers are ideal for storing and transporting food. They are durable, leakproof, and easy to clean. They come in various sizes and shapes, so you can find the perfect one for your needs. Here are some of the most common types of stainless steel food containers:

1. Food storage container sets. These sets come with various-sized containers, so you can easily store your food in one place.
2. Glass storage jars. These jars are perfect for storing small amounts of food. They are also easy to clean and sterilize.
3. Plastic storage containers. These containers are perfect for storing large quantities of food. They are durable, and they don't corrode or rust over time.
4. Stainless steel pots and pans. Stainless steel pots and pans are ideal for cooking and baking foods. They are resistant to heat and won't damage your food or cookware.
5. Stainless steel bowls and plates. These bowls and plates are perfect for serving food to customers or guests. They are dishwasher safe, so you can easily clean them afterward.

10.5 Safe Reheating Guidelines

You can safely reheat your prepped meals by following simple guidelines in the microwave, in the oven, or on the stovetop.

Safely Reheating Meals In The Microwave

While a microwave won't always produce the same results as an oven, using a microwave for reheating prepped meals is often much faster and more convenient. Here are a few general tips for getting the best results when reheating your prepped meals in a microwave oven.

Always Remove The Lids

There are many myths surrounding microwaving food. Some people believe you should never remove the lid of a microwave-safe food container because this will cause the heat from the microwaves to cook the food from the inside out. Others think it's necessary to keep the lid on to create a hot and moist environment for cooking your food. The truth is that neither of these practices is necessary - they can both be harmful.

The main problem with keeping the lid on is that it prevents steam from escaping. This steam heat cooks your food more quickly than if you left the oven door open. It also causes condensation inside the container, leading to bacteria growth. By removing the lid, you allow steam and moisture to escape, which reduces the chances of bacteria growth and gives your food a better chance of becoming nutrient-rich and delicious.

So what should you do? Always remove the lids when microwaving foods unless you have a reason not to (like adding ingredients). This will help reduce bacteria and make your food tastier and more nutritious!

Be Sure To Thaw Frozen Meals Before Reheating

Thawed foods should be placed in a single layer on a paper towel-lined plate and microwaved on high for 2 minutes or until heated through. Frozen food will heat up quickly and could reach dangerous temperatures. Instead, defrost your food before heating it in the oven.

Three Minutes On High Usually Does The Trick

As a general rule, microwaving refrigerated prepped meals for about 3 minutes on high should be sufficient for most of the recipes in this book. If possible, larger ingredients such as proteins should be removed from containers and reheated in the microwave first to ensure other foods don't become overcooked in the process. Also, ensure the food's surface is as smooth as possible to ensure even reheating.

Only Reheat Glass Containers Or Microwave Safe Ones

Microwave reheating guidelines can be tricky, but using glass containers can make the process safer. According to the Food and Drug Administration, microwaves are not meant to heat food above 455 °F. Additionally, heating food in a plastic container can release harmful chemicals into the food. By heating food in a glass container, you reduce the risk of harmful chemicals leaching into your food. Furthermore, using a glass container will also keep your microwaves clean. Alternatively, you may also opt for containers marked "Microwave Safe."

Safely Reheating Meals In An Oven Or On The Stovetop

Are you tired of cleaning up your microwave after using it to reheat food? There is a simple solution that you can use to help minimize the amount of mess that you make. Instead of using a dish, use a baking sheet. This will help to reduce the amount of grease and food particles that are created when microwaving food. Additionally, using a baking sheet will help to prevent the food from sticking to the bottom of the microwave oven. By following these simple guidelines, you can avoid cleaning your microwave often and create less of a mess in the process.

Reheat To The Same Temperature The Meal Was Prepared To

When reheating your meals, the meals should be reheated to the same temperatures they were originally cooked to, and for most recipes in this book, reheating your meals on the middle oven rack for 20 minutes in a preheated oven setto350°F(180°C) should be sufficient. Use a thermometer to check the meals every 5 minutes, after 10 minutes.

Use A Baking Sheet To Minimize The Mess

Whenever reheating a meal in the oven, place it on a baking tray lined with parchment paper. This will prevent any liquids that bubble over from the container from dripping onto the surface of your oven, which can create a mess.

Stick To The Stovetop For Certain Recipes

While a conventional oven or microwave oven will work for reheating the majority of the recipes in this book, some recipes that were originally prepared in a frying pan or in a pot, such as soups, are best reheated in a large frying pan or pot placed over medium heat on the stovetop.

Use A Thermometer To Check The Temperature

Whichever method you follow to reheat your meals, it’s best to check the internal temperature of the food to ensure it’s been reheated to the proper cooking temperature. A simple oven or kitchen thermometer is all you’ll need to do this.

11 BREAKFAST RECIPES

11.1 Bacon And Brie Omelet Wedges

Preparation Time: 10 minutes
Cooking Time: 10 minutes
Servings: 4

Ingredients:

- Dijon Mustard – 1 Tsp.
- Olive Oil – 2 Tbsp.
- Smoked Bacon – 7 Oz.
- Eggs – 6 Whole (Lightly Beaten)
- Chives, Snipped Up – Small Bunch
- Ounce Of Sliced Brie – 3 And ½ Oz. (Sliced)
- Red Wine Vinegar – 1 Tsp.
- Cucumber Sliced Up Diagonally – 1 Whole (Deseeded And Sliced)
- Radish – 7 Oz. (Sectioned)

Procedure:

1. Turn on your grill
2. Take a small-sized pan and add 1 tsp. of oil
3. Allow it to heat up over the grill
4. Add bacon and fry them until nice and crisp
5. Drain the bacon on kitchen paper
6. Take another non-sticky frying pan and place it over the grill
7. Heat up 2 tsp. of oil
8. Add bacon, eggs, and chives to the frying pan and sprinkle ground pepper
9. Cook over low heat until it is semi set
10. Carefully lay the Brie on top
11. Grill until the Brie has set and shows a golden texture
12. Remove the pan and cut the omelet up into wedges
13. Take a small bowl and create a salad by mixing olive oil, mustard, vinegar, and seasoning
14. Add cucumber and radish to the bowl
15. Mix well and serve it alongside the Omelet wedges
16. Enjoy!

Nutrition value per serving: Calories: 35 kcal, Fat: 31 g, Carbs: 3 g, Protein: 25 g, Sodium: 245 mg

11.2 Black Olive Breakfast Loaf

Preparation Time: 10 minutes
Cooking Time: 60 minutes
Servings: 4

Ingredients:

- Bread Flour – 3 Cups
- Active Dry Yeast – 2 Tsp.
- White Sugar – 2 Tbsp.
- Salt – 1 Tsp.
- Black Olives – ½ Cup (Chopped)
- Olive Oil – 3 Tbsp.
- Warm Water (110 Degree Fahrenheit) – 1 And ¼ Cups
- Cornmeal – 1 Tbsp.

Procedure:

1. Take a large-sized bowl and add flour, sugar, yeast, salt, black olives, water, and olive oil
2. Mix well to prepare the dough
3. Turn the dough onto a floured surface and knead it well for about 5-10 minutes until elastic
4. Keep it on the side and allow it to rise for about 45 minutes until it has doubled in size
5. Punch the dough down and knead again for 10 minutes
6. Allow it to rise for 30 minutes more
7. Round up the dough on the kneading board
8. Place upside down in a bowl and line it up with a lint-free, well flour towel
9. Allow it to rise until it has doubled in size
10. While the bread is rising up for the third and final time, take a pan and fill it up with water
11. Place it at the bottom of your oven
12. Pre-heat your oven to a temperature of 500°F
13. Turn the loaf out onto a sheet pan and lightly oil it
14. Dust with some cornmeal

15. Bake for about 15 minutes
16. Lower the heat to 375°F
17. Bake for another 30 minutes
18. Enjoy!

Nutrition value per serving: Calories: 138 kcal, Fat: 3 g, Carbs: 22 g, Protein: 3 g, Sodium: 245 mg

11.3 Mediterranean Bread With Melted Cheese

Preparation Time: 10 minutes
Cooking Time: 5 minutes
Servings: 4
Ingredients:

- Fresh parsley – ¼ cup (chopped)
- Black pepper – ¼ tsp.
- Salt- 1 tsp.
- Garlic clove – 1 (minced)
- Olive oil – 1 tbsp.
- Feta cheese – ¼ cup (crumbled)
- Mozzarella cheese – ½ cup (shredded)
- Bread – 1 loaf

Procedure:

1. Preheat the oven to 350 degrees.
2. Place loaf bread on a baking sheet and brush with olive oil. Sprinkle with garlic, salt, and pepper. Bake for 10 minutes or until the bread is golden brown.
3. Add mozzarella cheese, feta cheese, and parsley to the top of the bread, spreading them nicely, and bake for an additional 5 minutes or until the cheese is melted.
4. Serve warm.

Nutrition value per serving: Calories: 477 kcal, Fat: 25 g, Carbs: 45 g, Protein: 16 g, Sodium: 245 mg

11.4 Vegetarian Shepherd's Pie

Preparation Time: 20 minutes
Cooking Time: 30 minutes
Servings: 4
Ingredients:

- Olive oil – 1 tbsp.
- Onion – 1 whole (chopped)
- Green bell pepper 1 whole (chopped)
- Carrots – 1 whole (peeled and chopped)
- Celery Rib – ½ cup (chopped)
- Garlic cloves -4 (minced)
- Dried thyme – 1 tsp.
- Dried basil - ½ tsp.
- Black pepper – ¼ tsp.
- Tomatoes 14 oz. (diced)
- Red kidney beans – 10 oz. (rinsed and drained)
- Corn – 6 oz. (drained)
- Vegetable broth – 2 cups

Procedure:

1. Preheat the oven to 350 °F (175 degrees C).
2. Heat oil in a large skillet over medium heat. Add onion, bell pepper, carrots, celery rib, and garlic; cook until vegetables are tender.
3. Stir in thyme, basil, and black pepper.
4. Add tomatoes with their juice, kidney beans, corn, and flour. Bring to a boil; cook until thickened.
5. Pour mixture into a greased 9x13 inch baking dish. Bake for 30 minutes or until heated through.
6. Once the surface has a golden texture, serve and enjoy.

Nutrition value per serving: Calories: 552 kcal, Fat: 24 g, Carbs: 64 g, Protein: 20 g, Sodium: 245 mg

11.5 Fresh Watermelon And Arugula Meal

Preparation Time: 10 minutes
Cooking Time: 15 minutes
Servings: 4
Ingredients:
Salad

- Feta Cheese – 1/3 Cup (Crumbled)
- Arugula – 5 Cups
- Kalamata Olives - 1/3 Cup (Halved)
- Watermelon – 2 Cups (cubed)

Vinaigrette

- Salt and black Pepper – As Needed
- Extra Virgin Olive Oil – ¼ Cup
- Shallots – 1 Small (Chopped)
- Sherry Vinegar – 2 Tbsp.

Procedure:

1. Take a medium-sized bowl and add arugula, feta, olives, and cubed watermelon to prepare the salad by mixing them all together
2. Take a small measure cup and add all of the ingredients listed under vinaigrette ingredients and whisk well
3. Season with some salt and pepper
4. When you are ready to serve, whisk the vinaigrette a stir and drizzle half of the vinaigrette over the salad
5. Toss well
6. Add more vinaigrette to lightly coat up the arugula
7. Enjoy!

Nutrition value per serving: Calories: 234 kcal, Fat: 27 g, Carbs: 8 g, Protein: 8 g, Sodium: 245 mg

11.6 Morning Scrambled Pesto Eggs

Preparation Time: 10 minutes
Cooking Time: 5-7 minutes
Servings: 2
Ingredients:

- Large Eggs – 4 Whole
- Butter – 1 Tbsp.
- Pesto – 1 Tbsp.
- Creamed Coconut Milk – 2 Tbsp.
- Salt And Pepper- As Needed

Procedure:

1. In a mixing bowl, break the eggs and blend them together.
2. Add a touch of salt and pepper for seasoning.
3. Warm up a non-stick frying pan on low heat, then add the butter to melt.
4. Gently pour the whisked eggs into the heated pan.
5. Keep the heat low and consistently stir, incorporating the pesto into the eggs.
6. Take the pan off the heat once the eggs have reached a scrambled consistency.
7. Combine the creamed coconut milk with the scrambled eggs.
8. Place the pan back on low heat and cook for another 1-2 minutes, or until the eggs become creamy.
9. Serve hot and savor your meal!

Storage: It can be stored in the refrigerator for 2-3 days.

Nutrition value per serving: Calories: 361 kcal, Fat: 31 g, Carbs: 3 g, Protein: 17 g, Sodium: 300 mg

11.7 Egg And Acorn In A Hole

Preparation Time: 10 minutes
Cooking Time: 20 minutes
Servings: 4
Ingredients:

- Acorn Squash – 2 Whole
- Whole Eggs – 5 Whole
- Extra Virgin Olive Oil – 2 Tbsp.
- Salt – As Needed
- Pepper – As Needed
- Dates – 5 Whole (Pitted)
- Walnut – 8 Halves
- Parsley - A Bunch
- Maple Syrup – As Needed For Garnish

Procedure:

1. Pre-heat your oven to 375°F
2. Slice the squash crosswise and prepare 3 slices with holes in them
3. While slicing the squash, make sure that each slice has a measurement of ¾ inch thickness
4. Remove the seeds from the slices
5. Take a baking sheet and line it up with parchment paper
6. Transfer the slices to your baking sheet and season them with salt and pepper
7. Bake in your oven for 20 minutes
8. Chop the walnuts and dates on your cutting board
9. Take the baking dish out from the oven and drizzle slices with olive oil
10. Crack an egg into each of the holes in the slices and season with pepper and salt
11. Sprinkle the chopped walnuts on top
12. Bake for 10 minutes
13. Garnish with parsley and add maple syrup
14. Enjoy!

Nutrition value per serving: Calories: 200 kcal, Fat: 12 g, Carbs: 17 g, Protein: 8 g, Sodium: 245 mg

11.8 Dill And Tomato Frittata

Preparation Time: 10 minutes
Cooking Time: 30 - 40 minutes
Servings: 4
Ingredients:

- Salt And Pepper – To Taste
- Feta Cheese- ½ Cup (Chopped)
- Eggs – 8 Whole
- Fresh Dill – ¼ Cup (Chopped)
- Cherry Tomatoes – 3 Cups (Quartered)
- Red Pepper – 1 Whole (Diced)
- Garlic Cloves – 2 (Minced)
- Onion – 1 Whole (Diced)
- Olive Oil – 1 Tbsp.

Procedure:

1. Preheat your oven to 350 °F. Grease a 9x13-inch baking dish. In a large skillet over medium heat, add olive oil and heat the oil.
2. Add the onion and garlic and cook until softened, about 5 minutes. Add the red pepper and cook for an additional 2 minutes.
3. Add the tomatoes and dill and bring to a simmer. Remove from heat. Whisk the eggs in a large bowl.
4. Gradually whisk in the tomato mixture until well combined.
5. Pour the mixture into the prepared baking dish. Sprinkle with feta cheese and salt and black pepper to taste. Bake for 30 minutes or until firm.

Nutrition value per serving: Calories: 200 kcal, Fat: 15 g, Carbs: 6 g, Protein: 9 g, Sodium: 245 mg

11.9 Fancy Olive And Cheese Loaf

Preparation Time: 10 minutes
Cooking Time: 15 minutes
Servings: 8

Ingredients:

- Soft Butter – ½ Cup
- Mayo – ¼ Cup
- Garlic Powder – 1 Tsp.
- Onion Powder – 1 Tsp.
- Mozzarella Cheese – 2 Cups
- Black Olives – ½ Cup
- French Bread – 1 Loaf (Halved)

Procedure:

1. The oven should be pre-heated at 350 °F.
2. 2. In a mixing bowl, combine the butter and mayo and whisk until well combined.
3. Add onion powder and garlic powder
4. Stir in olives and cheese
5. Spread the whole mixture over French bread
6. Place them on your baking sheet and bake for 10-12 minutes
7. Increase the heat to broil and cook until the cheese has melted until the bread is golden brown

Storage: It can be stored in BPA Free container for around 4-5 days in the refrigerator and 1-2 months in the freezer.

Nutrition value per serving: Calories: 400 kcal, Fat: 23 g, Carbs: 34 g, Protein: 13 g, Sodium: 245 mg

11.10 Savory Pistachio Balls

Preparation Time: 10 minutes
Cooking Time: 10 minutes
Servings: 4

Ingredients:

- Raisins – ½ Cup
- Fennel Seeds – ½ Tsp. (Ground)
- Dates – 1 Cup (Pitted)
- Pistachios – ½ Cup (Unsalted)
- Pepper – Just A Pinch
- Salt – Just A Pinch
- Fresh Parsley – 1 Tsp.

Procedure:

1. Preheat oven to 375 °F (190 degrees C).
2. Line a baking sheet with parchment paper.
3. In a medium bowl, combine pistachios, salt, raisins, dates and pepper.
4. With your hands, work the mixture into 1-inch balls.
5. In a large skillet over medium heat, heat olive oil.
6. Add onion and cook until softened, about 5 minutes.
7. Add parsley and cook for 1 minute more.
8. Remove from heat and roll pistachio balls in onion mixture until coated.
9. Place on prepared baking sheet and repeat until all ingredients are used up.
10. Bake in oven for 10 minutes until golden
11. Enjoy!

Storage: It can be stored in BPA Free container for around 4-5 days in the refrigerator and 1-2 months in the freezer.

Nutrition value per serving: Calories: 528 kcal, Fat: 2 g, Carbs: 10 g, Protein: 2 g, Sodium: 245 mg

11.11 Roasted Almonds

Preparation Time: 10 minutes
Cooking Time: 20 minutes
Servings: 4
Ingredients:

- Almonds – 2 and ½ cups
- Cayenne – ¼ tsp.
- Coriander – ¼ tsp.
- Cumin – ¼ tsp.
- Chili powder – ¼ tbsp.
- Rosemary – 1 tbsp. (chopped)
- Maple syrup – 2 and ½ tbsp.
- Salt – just a pinch

Procedure:

1. Preheat oven to 350 °F.
2. Spread almonds on a baking sheet and bake for 10 minutes, or until lightly browned. In a large skillet over medium heat, heat olive oil.
3. Add garlic and cook for 1 minute.
4. Add oregano and cumin; season with salt and pepper, remaining herbs and spices, to taste. Cook for 2 minutes longer.
5. Toss well to ensure that everything is mixed
6. Enjoy!

Storage: It can be stored in BPA Free container for around 4-5 days in the refrigerator and 1-2 months in the freezer.

Nutrition value per serving: Calories: 528 kcal, Fat: 2 g, Carbs: 10 g, Protein: 2 g, Sodium: 245 mg

11.12 Chocolate Matcha Balls

Preparation Time: 10 minutes
Cooking Time: 5 minutes
Servings: 4
Ingredients:

- Unsweetened Cocoa Powder – 2 Tbsp.
- Oats, Gluten-Free – 3 Tbsp.
- Pine Nuts – ½ Cup
- Almonds – ½ Cup
- Dates – 1 Cup (Pitted)
- Matcha Powder – 2 Tbsp.

Procedure:

1. Add cocoa powder, oats, pine nuts, almonds, and dates into a food processor and process until well combined.
2. Place matcha powder in a small dish.
3. Make small balls from mixture and coat with matcha powder.
4. Enjoy or store in refrigerator until ready to eat.

Storage: It can be stored in BPA Free container for around 4-5 days in the refrigerator and 1-2 months in the freezer.

Nutrition value per serving: Calories: 528 kcal, Fat: 2 g, Carbs: 10 g, Protein: 2 g, Sodium: 245 mg

12 SALADS RECIPES

12.1 Blood Orange Vinaigrette Salad

Preparation Time: 10 minutes
Cooking Time: 0 minute
Servings: 4
Ingredients:
For Blood Orange Vinaigrette

- Extra Virgin Olive Oil – 1/3 Cup
- Fresh Blood Orange Juice – ½ Cup
- Red Wine Vinegar – 2 Tbsp.
- Fresh Ginger – 1 Tbsp. (Grated)
- Garlic Powder – 1 Tsp.
- Ground Sumac – 1 Tsp.
- Salt– As Needed
- Pepper– As Needed
- Mustard Oil – 1 tsp.

For Base Salad

- Vegetable Oil – 2/3 Cup
- Sumac – ½ Tsp.
- Shallots – 2 (Sliced)
- Salt – As Needed
- Raw Unsalted Almonds – 1/3 Cup
- Raw Sliced Almonds – 1/3 Cup
- Pita Bread – 2 Loaves
- Paprika – ½ Tsp.
- Frisee Lettuce – 3 Cups (Chopped)
- Dried Apricots – 1/3 Cup (Chopped)
- Blood Oranges – 1 To 2 (Peeled And Sliced)
- 4 Cups Of Baby Spinach – 4 Cups

Procedure:

1. Cut the blood orange in half crosswise and remove the seeds. Peel and chop the flesh.
2. In a small bowl, whisk together the red wine vinegar, Dijon mustard, and olive oil until well combined. Season with salt and pepper to taste.
3. Add the chopped blood orange to the vinaigrette and stir to combine.
4. Take another bowl and mix all the ingredients listed under salad, cover with vinaigrette and toss
5. Serve and enjoy!

Storage: Can be stored in airtight BPA Safe containers for 3-4 days in the refrigerator. However, not recommended to store in the freezer for a long time as it does not stay well.

Nutrition value per serving: Calories: 528 kcal, Fat: 2 g, Carbs: 10 g, Protein: 2 g, Sodium: 245 mg

12.2 Mediterranean Tabouli Salad

Preparation Time: 10 minutes
Cooking Time: 0 minute
Servings: 4
Ingredients:

- Salt As Needed – As Needed
- Romaine Lettuce Leaves - As Needed
- Roma Tomatoes– 4 Whole (Chopped)
- Mint Leaves– 12 To 15 Leaves (Chopped)
- Lime Juice – 3 To 4 Tbsp.
- Green Onions (With White And Green Parts) – 4 Whole (Chopped)
- Fresh Parsley (Washed Up And Finely Chopped) – 2 Bunch
- Extra Virgin Olive Oil – 3-4 Tbsp.
- Extra Fine Bulgar Wheat – ½ Cup
- Cucumber – 1 Whole (Chopped)
- Kidney Beans – 1 cup (Cooked)
- Cilantro – As Deeded
- Pepper – as needed

Procedure:

1. Take a mixing bowl and add lime juice and olive oil to make the dressing
2. Take a salad bowl and add all of the remaining ingredients. Toss them well to mix thoroughly.
3. Serve chilled or at room temperature.

Storage: Can be stored in airtight BPA Safe containers for 3-4 days in the refrigerator. However, not recommended to store in the freezer for a long time as it does not stay well.

Nutrition value per serving: Calories: 528 kcal, Fat: 2 g, Carbs: 10 g, Protein: 2 g, Sodium: 245 mg

12.3 Kidney Beans Cilantro Salad

Preparation Time: 10 minutes
Cooking Time: 0 minute
Servings: 4

Ingredients:

- Kidney Beans (Drained And Rinsed) – 15 Oz.
- English Cucumber Chopped Up – ½ Cup (Chopped)
- Heirloom Tomatoes – 1 Medium Sized (Chopped)
- Fresh Cilantro Bunch (Stems Removed)
- Onion – 1 Whole (Chopped)
- Lime – 1 Whole
- Dijon Mustard – 3 Tbsp.
- Fresh Garlic Paste – ½ Tsp.
- Sumac – 1 Tsp.
- Salt -As Needed
- Pepper– As Needed

Procedure:

1. Take a medium-sized bowl and add Kidney beans, chopped-up veggies, and cilantro
2. Take a small bowl and make the vinaigrette by adding lime juice, oil, fresh garlic paste, pepper, mustard, and sumac
3. Pour the vinaigrette over the salad and give it a nice stir
4. Add some salt and pepper
5. Cover it up and allow it to chill for half an hour
6. Serve!

Storage: Can be stored in airtight BPA Safe containers for 3-4 days in the refrigerator. However, not recommended to store in the freezer for a long time as it does not stay well.

Nutrition value per serving: Calories: 528 kcal, Fat: 2 g, Carbs: 10 g, Protein: 2 g, Sodium: 245 mg

12.4 Simple Medi Salad

Preparation Time: 10 minutes
Cooking Time: 0 minute
Servings: 4

Ingredients:

- Romaine Lettuce – 1 Whole (Chopped)
- Roma Tomatoes – 3 Whole (Diced)
- English Cucumber – 1 Whole (Diced)
- Onions – 1 Whole
- Curly Parsley– ½ Cup (Chopped)
- Olive Oil – 2 Tbsp.
- Large Lemon – ½ A Lemon
- Garlic Powder – 1 Tsp.
- Salt – As Needed
- Pepper– As Needed

Procedure:

1. Wash the vegetable thoroughly
2. Prepare them as indicated in the ingredients section
3. Take a large-sized bowl and add vegetables, olive oil, spices, and lemon juice
4. Toss well and transfer them to your serving bowl
5. Enjoy fresh!

Storage: Can be stored in airtight BPA Safe containers for 3-4 days in the refrigerator. However, not recommended to store in the freezer for a long time as it does not stay well.

Nutrition value per serving: Calories: 528 kcal, Fat: 2 g, Carbs: 10 g, Protein: 2 g, Sodium: 245 mg

12.5 Tuna And Dijon Salad

Preparation Time: 10 minutes
Cooking Time: 0 minute
Servings: 4
Ingredients:
For Base recipe

- Genova Tuna Dipped In Olive Oil – 5 Oz.
- Celery Stalks– 2 And ½ Stalks (Chopped)
- English Cucumber – ½ A Cucumber (Chopped)
- Radishes- 4 To 5 Whole (Stems Removed, Chopped)
- Green Onions– 3 Whole (Chopped)
- Red Onion– ½ A Medium Sized (Chopped)
- Kalamata Olives – ½ Cup (Halved)
- Parsley– 1 Bunch (Chopped)
- Fresh Mint Leaves– 10 To 15 Sprigs (Stems Removed, Chopped)
- Heirloom Tomatoes – 5 Slices
- Pita Pockets For Serving - For Serving

For Zesty Dijon Mustard Vinaigrette

- Dijon Mustard – 2 And ½ Tsp.
- Zest Of Lime – 1 Piece (Zest)
- Juice Of Lime – 1 And ½ (Juiced)
- Olive Oil – 1/3 Cup
- Sumac – ½ Tsp.
- Salt – Pinch
- Pepper– As Needed
- Crushed Red Pepper Flakes – ½ Tsp. (Crushed)

Procedure:

1. Prepare the Zest Mustard Vinaigrette by taking a small bowl and adding all of the ingredients listed under Zesty Dijon Mustard vinaigrette. Stir well.
2. For the Tuna salad, take a large-sized bowl and add 3 cans of 5-ounce Genova Tuna (or your preferred brand) alongside the chopped vegetables, chopped up fresh parsley, mint leaves, and Kalamata olives
3. Mix well using a spoon
4. Dress the tuna salad with the prepared vinaigrette
5. Mix again until the tuna salad is properly coated with the vinaigrette
6. Cover and allow it to chill for 30 minutes
7. Once done, give the salad a toss and serve with a side of pita chips or pita bread and some sliced-up heirloom tomatoes!
8. Enjoy!

Storage: Can be stored in airtight BPA Safe containers for 3-4 days in the refrigerator. However, not recommended to store in the freezer for a long time as it does not stay well.

Nutrition value per serving: Calories: 528 kcal, Fat: 2 g, Carbs: 10 g, Protein: 2 g, Sodium: 245 mg

12.6 Arugula And Garlic Avocado Vinaigrette

Preparation Time: 10 minutes
Cooking Time: 0 minute
Servings: 4
Ingredients:
For Base recipe

- Shelled Fava Beans – 1 And ½ Cups
- Persian Cucumbers – 3 Whole (Chopped)
- Packed Grape Tomatoes – 2 Cups (Halved)
- Packed Baby Arugula -4 Cups
- Jalapeno Pepper – 1 Whole (Sliced)
- Green Onions– 4 Whole (Chopped)
- Avocado – 1 Whole

For Lemon-Honey Vinaigrette

- Salt– As Needed
- Pepper - As Needed
- Juice Of Lemon – 1 And 1/2
- Garlic Clove – 1 Clove (Chopped)
- Extra Virgin Olive Oil – ½ Cup
- Cilantro – 2 Tbsp. (Chopped)
- Chopped Fresh Mint - 2 Tbsp. (Chopped)

Procedure:

1. Prepare your ingredients as directed above
2. Take a small-sized bowl and add the ingredients listed under the vinaigrette

3. Whisk them well to prepare the vinaigrette
4. Take a large-sized mixing bowl and the remaining ingredients from the base ingredients section, except for avocado
5. Dress the salad with garlic herb vinaigrette and finely toss them
6. Peel your avocado at this point and core it up
7. Chop it up and add the avocado to the salad as well
8. Divide the whole salad among four bowls
9. Enjoy!

Storage: Can be stored in airtight BPA Safe containers for 3-4 days in the refrigerator. However, not recommended to store in the freezer for a long time as it does not stay well.

Nutrition value per serving: Calories: 528 kcal, Fat: 2 g, Carbs: 10 g, Protein: 2 g, Sodium: 245 mg

12.7 Homely Fattoush Salad

Preparation Time: 10 minutes
Cooking Time: 0 minute
Servings: 4
Ingredients:
For Base recipe

- Pita Bread – 2 Loaves
- Extra Virgin Olive Oil – As Needed
- Tsp. Of Sumac – ½ Tsp.
- Salt– As Needed
- Pepper - As Needed
- Romaine Lettuce Chopped Up – 1 Whole Heart (Chopped)
- English Cucumber – 1 Whole (Chopped)
- Roma Tomatoes – 5 Whole (Chopped)
- Onions– 5 Whole (Chopped)
- Radishes– 5 Whole (Thinly Sliced)
- Fresh Parsley Leaves (Stems Removed) – 2 Cups (Chopped)
- Fresh Mint Leaves - 1 Cup (Chopped)

For Lime Vinaigrette

- Sumac – 1 Tsp.
- Ground Allspice – ¼ Tsp.
- Ground Cinnamon – ¼ Tsp.
- Juice Of Lime – 1 And ½
- Bottle Of Extra Virgin Olive Oil – 1/3 A Bottle
- Salt– As Needed
- Pepper– As Needed

Procedure:

1. Add your pita bread to your toasted and toast them until they are crisp but not browned
2. Take a large-sized pan and place it over medium heat
3. Add 3 tablespoons of olive oil and heat it up
4. Break the toasted pita into pieces and add them to the oil
5. Fry until browned, making sure to toss them from time to time
6. Add salt, ½ a tsp. of sumac, and pepper
7. Remove the pita from the heat and place them on a paper towel to drain them
8. Take a large-sized mixing bowl and add chopped-up lettuce, tomatoes, cucumber, and green onions with sliced-up parsley and radish
9. Make the lime vinaigrette by taking a bowl and mixing all of the ingredients listed under vinaigrette
10. Toss the salad with vinaigrette very gently
11. Add pita chips on top and some additional sumac
12. Give it a final toss, and enjoy!

Storage: Can be stored in airtight BPA Safe containers for 3-4 days in the refrigerator. However, not recommended to store in the freezer for a long time as it does not stay well.

Nutrition value per serving: Calories: 528 kcal, Fat: 2 g, Carbs: 10 g, Protein: 2 g, Sodium: 245 mg

12.8 Roasted Beet And Kale Salad

Preparation Time: 10 minutes
Cooking Time: 30 minute
Servings: 4
Ingredients:
For Base recipe

- Seasonings: olive oil, pepper, and salt as needed
- Bunch Of Kale– 1 Bunch (Washed And Dried)
- Washed Beets– 5 Whole (Washed, Peeled, and Dried)
- Dried Rosemary – ½ Tsp.
- Garlic Powder – ½ Tsp.
- Red Onion – ¼ Medium (Thinly Sliced)
- Almonds - 2 Tbsp. (Slivered)

For Lemon-Honey Vinaigrette

- Lemon Juice – 1 And 1/2
- Garlic Powder – ¼ Tsp.
- Olive Oil – ¼ Cup
- Honey – ¼ Cup
- Dried Rosemary – 1 Tsp.
- Salt– As Needed
- Pepper– As Needed

Procedure:

1. Pre-heat your oven to a temperature of 400 °F
2. Toss kale, onion, and beets with rosemary, garlic powder, and almonds
3. Take a small-sized bowl and add the ingredients for the lemon honey vinaigrette. Mix well until you have a nice dressing. Drizzle the dressing over your prepared kale.
4. Transfer the kale to a baking sheet lined with parchment paper. Transfer to oven.
5. Roast for 20-25 minutes, stirring once, on a baking sheet. The dish can be served at room temperature or warmed to your preference.

Storage: Can be stored in airtight BPA Safe containers for 3-4 days in the refrigerator. However, not recommended to store in the freezer for a long time as it does not stay well.

Nutrition value per serving: Calories: 528 kcal, Fat: 2 g, Carbs: 10 g, Protein: 2 g, Sodium: 245 mg

12.9 Pearl Couscous Salad

Preparation Time: 10 minutes
Cooking Time: 0 minute
Servings: 4
Ingredients:
For Lemon Dill Vinaigrette

- Juice Of Large Sized Lemon – 1 Whole (Juiced)
- Extra Virgin Olive Oil – 1/3 Cup
- Dill Weed – 1 Tsp.
- Garlic Powder - 1 Tsp.
- Salt– As Needed
- Pepper – As Needed

For Israeli Couscous

- Pearl Couscous – 2 Cups
- Extra Virgin Olive Oil – As Needed
- Red Onion – 1 Cup (Sliced)
- Cilantro – 1 Bunch (Chopped)
- Smoked Paprika – 1 Tsp.
- Salt And Black Pepper – As Needed

Procedure:

1. In a medium bowl, combine the couscous, red onion, parsley, cilantro, smoked paprika, salt, and black pepper; stir to combine.
2. Prepare the lemon dill vinaigrette by taking a small-sized bowl and adding the ingredients listed under Lemon Dill Vinaigrette; stir well
3. Pour the mix over the Israeli Couscous mix and toss
4. Serve at room temperature or chilled.

Storage: Can be stored in airtight BPA Safe containers for 3-4 days in the refrigerator. However, not recommended to store in the freezer for a long time as it does not stay well.

Nutrition value per serving: Calories: 528 kcal, Fat: 2 g, Carbs: 10 g, Protein: 2 g, Sodium: 245 mg

12.10 Sweet Broad Bean Pomegranate Mix

Preparation Time: 10 minutes
Cooking Time: 0 minute
Servings: 4

Ingredients:

- Pumpkin Seeds – 2 Tbsp.
- Pomegranate Seeds – 1 Cup
- Parsley – Small Bunch (Chopped)
- Mint – Small Bunch (Chopped)
- Large Handful Of Watercress - Large Handful
- Frozen Broad Beans – 1 And ½ Cups
- Fennel Bulb - 1 Whole (Core Removed, Thinly Sliced)
- Bulgar Wheat – 1 Cup

For Dressing

- Zest Of Lemon – 1 Whole Lemon
- Juice Of Lemon - 1 Lemon (Juiced)
- Extra Virgin Rapeseed Oil – 5 Tbsp.
- Dijon Mustard - 1 Tbsp.
- Cider Vinegar – 2 Tbsp.

Procedure:

1. Take a bowl and add Bulgar Wheat alongside a bit of salt
2. Take a kettle and heat up some water and bring to a boil
3. Pour the boiling water over the Bulgar and allow it to sit for 10 minutes
4. Lock up the lid and give it a nice shake
5. Uncover and drain
6. Tip in the Bulgar wheat into a bowl
7. Add fennel, pomegranate, herbs, pumpkin seeds and broad beans
8. Take a jar and add the ingredients listed under dressing, mix them well and pour over Bulgar.
9. Toss well
10. Top up with some salad leaves (watercress)
11. Drizzle with the dressing
12. Enjoy!

Storage: Can be stored in airtight BPA Safe containers for 3-4 days in the refrigerator. However, not recommended to store in the freezer for a long time as it does not stay well.

Nutrition value per serving: Calories: 355 kcal, Fat: 13 g, Carbs: 38 g, Protein: 11 g, Sodium: 245 mg

13 SOUPS RECIPES

13.1 Pear And Cinnamon Squash Soup

Preparation Time: 10 minutes
Cooking Time: 20 minutes
Servings: 4

Ingredients:

- Greek Yogurt – ¼ Cup
- White Kidney Beans – ½ Cup
- Salt – ½ Tsp.
- Black Pepper – ½ Tsp.
- Butternut Squash – 1 Small (Peeled Into 1 Inch Pieces)
- Pear – 1 Small (Peeled And Cored)
- Yellow Onion – 1 Small (Diced)
- Cinnamon – 1 Stick
- Dried Oregano – 1 Tsp.
- Low Sodium Chicken Stock – 2 Cups
- Garlic Cloves – 2 Large Sized
- Extra Virgin Olive Oil – 2 Tbsp.
- Oregano – 2 Tbsp.
- Parsley – 2tbsp. (Chopped)
- Walnuts – 2 Tbsp.

Procedure:

1. In a large pot or Dutch oven, heat the olive oil over medium heat.
2. Add the onion and cook until softened, about 5 minutes.
3. Add the butternut squash, pears, cinnamon, and stock. Bring to a boil and then reduce the heat to a low simmer.
4. Cook until the vegetables are tender, about 20 minutes.
5. Purée the soup in a blender or food processor until smooth. Season with salt and pepper to taste. Serve hot.
6. Season with oregano and parsley, and add some walnuts on top. Serve and enjoy!

Storage: It can be stored in BPA Safe container or pots for up to 3-4 days in the fridge and 2 months in the freezer.

Nutrition value per serving: Calories: 200 kcal, Fat: 10 g, Carbs: 12 g, Protein: 3 g, Sodium: 300 mg, Potassium:

13.2 Mediterranean Pepper Soup

Preparation Time: 10 minutes
Cooking Time: 30 minutes
Servings: 6

Ingredients:

- Uncooked Rice – ¼ Cup
- Onion – 1 Whole (Chopped)
- Green Pepper – 1 Large (Chopped)
- Tomato – 1 Large (Chopped)
- Lean Ground Beef – 1 Lb. (Ground)
- Garlic Cloves – 2 (Minced)
- Parsley (Additional For Garnish) – 2 Tbsp. (Chopped)
- Olive Oil – 2 Tbsp.
- Tomato Paste – 2 Tbsp.
- Beef Broth – 4 Cups
- Salt And Pepper – As Needed
- Oregano – 1 tbsp.
- Cumin – 1 tsp.
- Red Wine Vinegar – ¼ cup

Procedure:

1. In a large pot, sauté onions, green pepper, ground beef, garlic cloves, and garlic in olive oil over medium heat until softened. Add the tomatoes with their juice, oregano, cumin, salt and black pepper and uncooked rice.
2. Bring to a boil then reduce heat and simmer for 30 minutes. Add beef broth and red wine vinegar.
3. Simmer for 10 more minutes or until heated through. Ladle into bowls and top with parsley leaves.
4. Serve hot, and enjoy!

Storage: It can be stored in BPA Safe container or pots for up to 3-4 days in the fridge and 2 months in the freezer.

Nutrition value per serving: Calories: 162 kcal, Fat: 3 g, Carbs: 12 g, Protein: 21 g, Sodium: 250 mg

13.3 Mediterranean Tomato Soup

Preparation Time: 10 minutes
Cooking Time: 25 minute
Servings: 4
Ingredients:

- Red Pepper Flakes – ½ Tsp.
- Coconut Milk – 14 Oz.
- Tomatoes – 15 Oz. (Diced)
- Plum Tomatoes – 28 Oz. (Diced)
- Coriander – 1 Tsp. (Ground)
- Cumin – 1 Tsp. (Ground)
- Red Curry Powder – 1 Tsp.
- Salt (Extra For Taste If Needed) – 1 Tsp.
- Yellow Onions – 2 Medium (Sliced)
- Curry Powder – 2 Tsp.
- Olive Oil - 4 Tbsp.
- Water (Vegetable Broth Or Chicken Broth Also Usable) – 5 And ½ Cups

Procedure:

1. In a large pot or Dutch oven over medium heat, sauté tomatoes, plum tomatoes, and yellow onions well
2. Add oregano and thyme and other spices and stir well
3. Add broth and oil and bring the mixture to a boil
4. Lower down the heat and simmer for about 30 minutes or until the lentils are cooked through. Serve hot.

Storage: It can be stored in BPA Safe container or pots for up to 3-4 days in the fridge and 2 months in the freezer.

Nutrition value per serving: Calories: 74 kcal, Fat: 0.7 g, Carbs: 16 g, Protein: 2 g, Sodium: 300 mg

13.4 Classic Tuscan Veggie Soup

Preparation Time: 10 minutes
Cooking Time: 20 minutes
Servings: 4
Ingredients:

- Black Pepper – ¼ Tsp.
- Salt – ½ Tsp.
- Onion – ½ An Onion (Diced)
- Garlic Clove – 1 Whole (Minced)
- Zucchini – 1 Small (Diced)
- Fresh Thyme Leaves – 1 Tbsp. (Chopped)
- Olive Oil – 1 Tbsp.
- Low Sodium Cannellini Beans (Drained And Rinsed) – 15 Oz.
- Freshly Grated Parmesan – 1/3 Cup
- Tomatoes – 14 Oz. (Diced)
- Baby Spinach Leaves – 2 Cups. (Chopped)
- Carrots – 2 Whole (Diced)
- Celery – 2 Stalks (Diced)
- Fresh Sage – 2 Tsp. (Chopped)
- Low Sodium Chicken Broth – 32 Oz.

Procedure:

1. Take a small-sized bowl and mash half of your beans using the back of your spoons
2. Keep it on the side
3. Take a large-sized soup pot and place it over medium-high heat
4. Add oil and allow it to heat up
5. Add carrots, onion, celery, garlic, zucchini, thyme, ½ a tsp. of salt, sage, ¼ tsp. of pepper, and cook well for about 5 minutes until the vegetables are tender
6. Add broth and tomatoes (with the juice) and bring the whole mixture to a boil
7. Add beans (both mashed and whole) alongside spinach
8. Cook for 3 minutes until the spinach has wilted
9. Serve with toppings of Parmesan
10. Enjoy!

Storage: It can be stored in BPA Safe container or pots for up to 3-4 days in the fridge and 2 months in the freezer.

Nutrition value per serving: Calories: 140 kcal, Fat: 9 g, Carbs: 21 g, Protein: 10 g, Sodium: 340 mg

13.5 Excellent Mediterranean Lemon Chicken Soup With Turmeric

Preparation Time: 10 minutes
Cooking Time: 40 minute
Servings: 4
Ingredients:

- Lemons (zest and juice) – 2 whole
- Fresh parsley – ½ Cup (Chopped)
- Fresh dill – ¼ Cup (chopped)
- Baby spinach – 2 cups
- Turmeric – 1/2 tsp.
- Aleppo pepper – 1 tsp.
- Coriander – 1 tsp.
- Carrot – 2 whole (peeled and sliced)
- Extra virgin olive oil – as needed
- Garlic cloves – 4 large (2 minced and 2 whole)
- Yellow Onion – 1 whole (Quartered)
- Chicken breast – 1 lb. (Boneless)

Procedure:

1. Take a large-sized Dutch oven and add 6 cups of water alongside the chicken.
2. Season the mix generously with salt and pepper, add Onion and garlic and bring the whole mix to a boil over medium-high heat.
3. Once the water has started to boil, lower the heat to simmer and let it cook for 15-20 minutes until the chicken is thoroughly cooked
4. Once done, remove the chicken from the pot and shred it using forks
5. Strain the remaining broth using a fine metal mesh/strainer and pour it into a large-sized bowl
6. Discard the whole garlic and Onion
7. Wipe the pot and return it back to medium heat
8. Add 2-3 tablespoons of olive oil and let it heat up
9. Add minced garlic, spices, and other vegetables except for spinach, parsley, and dill
10. Add the now shredded chicken to the pot, and stir the whole mixture well
11. Add the reserved broth and bring the mixture to a boil. Once boiling point is reached, remove the heat and cook for about 20 minutes, partly covered
12. Stir in herbs and spinach alongside the zest and juice of a lemon
13. Mix and serve!

Storage: It can be stored in BPA Safe container or pots for up to 3-4 days in the fridge and 2 months in the freezer.

Nutrition value per serving: Calories: 170 kcal, Fat: 3 g, Carbs: 9 g, Protein: 25 g, Sodium: 72 mg, Potassium: 512 mg

13.6 Homely Sweet Potato Soup

Preparation Time: 10 minutes
Cooking Time: 30 minutes
Servings: 4
Ingredients:

- Coriander – ½ Tsp. (Ground)
- Chili – ¼ Tsp. (Ground)
- Cinnamon – ¼ Tsp. (Ground)
- Salt – ¼ Tsp.
- Cumin – ½ Tsp. (Ground)
- Onion – 1 Large (Chopped)
- Sweet Potato – 1 Lb. (Peeled And Cut)
- Garlic – 2 Cloves (Crushed)
- Chicken Stock – 2 Cups
- Extra Virgin Olive Oil – 2 Tbsp.
- Coriander - As Needed For Garnish
- Freshly Parsley – As Needed For Garnish
- Low Fat Crème Fraiche - As Needed For Garnish

Procedure:

1. In a soup pot over medium heat, heat the oil. Add the onion and garlic and cook until softened, about 5 minutes.
2. Add the rest of the vegetables alongside and cook them for 2-3 minutes until crispy, making sure to add the spices as well

3. Add the broth and ring the mix to a boil
4. Simmer until the vegetables are tender when pierced with a fork, about 20 minutes. Garnish with crème Fraiche on top, and enjoy!

Storage: It can be stored in BPA Safe container or pots for up to 3-4 days in the fridge and 2 months in the freezer.

Nutrition value per serving: Calories: 300 kcal, Fat: 10 g, Carbs: 15 g, Protein: 25 g, Sodium: 347 mg

13.7 Lovely Onion Soup

Preparation Time: 10 minutes
Cooking Time:250 minute
Servings: 4

Ingredients:

- Red Wine – 1 cup
- Brandy – 1 measure
- Butter – 1 oz.
- Parmesan Cheese – 1 oz. (grated)
- Flour – 1 tbsp.
- Brown Sugar – 1 tsp.
- Provence Herbs De Provence – 1 tsp.
- Vegetable Stock – 2 cups
- Large Onions – 2 whole (sliced)
- Olive Oil – 2 tbsp.
- Strong Cheese – 4 oz. (grated)
- Stale Bread – 4 Slices
- Salt and Pepper – as needed

Procedure:

1. Place a pan on medium-high heat.
2. Allow the butter and oil to warm up before adding.
3. Add onions and sugar
4. Cook until the onions and golden brown
5. Pour brandy and flambe, making sure to keep stirring it until the flames are out
6. Add plain flour and herbs de Provence and keep stirring well
7. Add stock and red wine (not all at once, bit by bit)
8. Season well and simmer for 20 minutes, making sure to add water if the soup becomes too thick
9. Ladle the soup into bowls
10. Slices of stale bread should be placed on top.
11. Add strong cheese
12. Sprinkle some parmesan over the top.
13. Place the bowls under a hot grill or in an oven until the cheese has melted
14. Serve immediately!

Storage: It can be stored in BPA Safe container or pots for up to 3-4 days in the fridge and 2 months in the freezer.

Nutrition value per serving: Calories: 55 kcal, Fat: 20 g, Carbs: 8 g, Protein: 6 g, Sodium: 222 mg

14 BEANS RECIPES

14.1 Black Bean With Mangoes

Preparation Time: 10 minutes
Cooking Time: 10 minute
Servings: 4
Ingredients:

- Coconut Oil – 2 Tbsp.
- Onion– 1 Whole (Chopped)
- Black Beans- 15 Oz. (Drained And Rinsed)
- Chili Powder – 1 Tbsp.
- Salt – 1 Tsp.
- Freshly Ground Black Pepper – ¼ Tsp.
- Water – 1 Cup
- Mangoes– 2 Whole (Sliced)
- Fresh Cilantro, Divided - ¼ Cup (Chopped)
- Scallions, Divided – ¼ Cup (Sliced)

Procedure:

1. Preheat the oven to 375 °F (190 degrees C).
2. In a bowl, combine black beans, red onion, mango, and olive oil.
3. Spread mixture in a single layer on a baking sheet and roast for 20 minutes, or until vegetables are tender.
4. Stir in cumin, chili powder, and salt; lime juice to taste. Serve warm.

Nutrition value per serving: Calories: 528 kcal, Fat: 2 g, Carbs: 10 g, Protein: 2 g, Sugar: 200 mg, Potassium: 100 mg

14.2 Italian Cannellini Beans

Preparation Time: 10 minutes
Cooking Time: minute
Servings: 415
Ingredients:

- Extra-Virgin Olive Oil – 2 Tsp.
- Onion – ½ Cup (Minced)
- Red Wine Vinegar – ¼ Cup
- No-Salt-Added Tomato Paste – 12 Oz.
- Raw Honey - 2 Tbsp.
- Water – ½ Cup
- Ground Cinnamon – ¼ Tsp. (Ground)
- Cannellini Beans – 15 Oz.

Procedure:

1. Heat the olive oil in a saucepan over medium heat until shimmering.
2. Add the onion and sauté for 5 minutes or until translucent.
3. Pour in the red wine vinegar, tomato paste, honey, and water.
4. Sprinkle with cinnamon. Stir to mix well.
5. Reduce the heat to low, then pour all the beans into the saucepan. Cook for 10 more minutes. Stir constantly.
6. Serve immediately.

Storage: It can be stored in airtight BPA Safe containers for around 4-5 days in the refrigerator and 4-6 months in the freezer.

Nutrition value per serving: Calories: 528 kcal, Fat: 2 g, Carbs: 10 g, Protein: 2 g, Sugar: 200 mg, Potassium: 100 mg

14.3 Mashed Beans And Cumin

Preparation Time: 10 minutes
Cooking Time: 10 minute
Servings: 4

Ingredients:

- Extra-Virgin Olive Oil, Plus Extra For Serving – 1 Tbsp.
- Garlic – 2 Cloves (Minced)
- Ground Cumin – 1 Tsp.
- Fava beans – 15 Oz.
- Tahini – 2 Tbsp.
- Lemon Juice, Plus Lemon Wedges For Serving – 2 Tbsp. (Juiced)
- Salt And Pepper – To Taste
- 1 Tomato– 1 Whole (Cored And Cut)
- Small Onion– 1 Whole (Chopped)
- Fresh Parsley – 2 Tbsp. (Chopped)

Procedure:

1. In a large bowl, combine all of the listed ingredients.
2. Bring the mix to a boil and simmer for 10-15 minutes until cooked
3. Serve warm or cold

Storage: It can be stored in airtight BPA Safe containers for around 4-5 days in the refrigerator and 4-6 months in the freezer.

Nutrition value per serving: Calories: 528 kcal, Fat: 2 g, Carbs: 10 g, Protein: 2 g, Sugar: 200 mg, Potassium: 100 mg

14.4 Turkish Canned Pinto Beans Salad

Preparation Time: 10 minutes
Cooking Time: 0 minute
Servings: 4

Ingredients:

- Olive Oil, Divided – ¼ Cup
- Garlic Cloves– 2 Cloves (Peeled and Crushed)
- Pinto Beans, Rinsed – 15 Oz.
- Water – 1 Tbsp.
- Salt And Pepper– As Needed
- Tahini – ¼ Cup
- Lemon Juice – 2 Tbsp.
- Aleppo Pepper, Plus Extra For Serving- 1 Tbsp.
- Cherry Tomatoes, Halved – 8oz. (Halved)
- Onion– ¼ An Onion (Sliced)
- Fresh Parsley Leaves – ¼ Cup
- Toasted Sesame Seeds – 1 Tbsp. (Toasted)

Procedure:

1. In a large salad bowl, combine all of the listed ingredients
2. Toss to combine. Serve chilled or at room temperature.

Storage: It can be stored in airtight BPA Safe containers for around 4-5 days in the refrigerator and 4-6 months in the freezer.

Nutrition value per serving: Calories: 528 kcal, Fat: 2 g, Carbs: 10 g, Protein: 2 g, Sugar: 200 mg, Potassium: 100 mg

14.5 Fava And Garbanzo Beans Platter

Preparation Time: 10 minutes
Cooking Time: 10 minutes
Servings: 4

Ingredients:

- Garbanzo Beans, Rinsed And Drained - 1 Lb.
- Fava Beans, Rinsed And Drained – 15 Oz.
- Water – 3 Cups
- Lemon Juice – ½ Cup
- Garlic – 3 Cloves (Peeled And Minced)
- Salt – 1 Tsp.
- Extra-Virgin Olive Oil – 2 Tbsp.

Procedure:

1. In a pot over medium heat, cook the beans in water for 10 minutes.
2. Drain the beans and transfer them to a bowl. Reserve 1 cup of the liquid from the cooked beans.
3. Add Salt, lemon juice, and chopped garlic to a bowl. Mix thoroughly.
4. About half of the beans should be mashed with a potato masher.
5. Add the prepared lemon dressing to the bowl with beans
6. Give the mixture one more stir to make sure the beans are evenly mixed.
7. Drizzle with the olive oil and serve.

Storage: It can be stored in airtight BPA Safe containers for around 4-5 days in the refrigerator and 4-6 months in the freezer.

Nutrition value per serving: Calories: 528 kcal, Fat: 2 g, Carbs: 10 g, Protein: 2 g, Sugar: 200 mg, Potassium: 100 mg

14.6 Bulgar Pilaf With Garbanzo Beans

Preparation Time: 10 minutes
Cooking Time: 20 minutes
Servings: 4

Ingredients:

- Extra-Virgin Olive Oil - 2 Tbsp.
- Onion – 1 Whole (Chopped)
- Garbanzo Beans– 1 Lb. (Rinsed And Drained)
- Bulgur Wheat - 2 Cups (Rinsed And Drained)
- Salt and pepper – 1 And ½ Tsp.
- Cinnamon – ½ Tsp.
- Water – 2 Cups
- Tomato Paste – 1 And ½ Cups
- Fresh parsley – 1 tsp.
- Fresh thyme – 1 tsp.

Procedure:

1. Preheat the oven to 350 °F (175 degrees C).
2. In a large bowl, combine bulgur, garbanzo beans, parsley, onion, garlic, oil, and thyme; season with salt and pepper. Mix well.
3. Pour mixture into an 8x8 inch baking dish. Bake for 25 minutes or until heated through.
4. In a small saucepan over medium heat, bring broth to a boil. Add tomato paste; cook for 2 minutes or until bubbly. Pour over pilaf; serve warm.

Storage: It can be stored in airtight BPA Safe containers for around 4-5 days in the refrigerator and 4-6 months in the freezer.

Nutrition value per serving: Calories: 528 kcal, Fat: 2 g, Carbs: 10 g, Protein: 2 g, Sugar: 200 mg, Potassium: 100 mg

14.7 Mediterranean Beans And Veggie

Preparation Time: 10 minutes
Cooking Time: 0 minute
Servings: 4

Ingredients:

- Tomatoes With Juice – 14 Oz. (Diced)
- Kidney Beans, Drained And Rinsed – 15 Oz. (Cooked)
- Black Beans, Drained And Rinsed – 15 oz. (Cooked)
- Green Olives– 2 Tbsp. (Chopped)
- Vegetable Broth, Plus More As Needed – ¼ Cup
- Extra-Virgin Olive Oil – 1 Tsp.
- Garlic – 2 Cloves (Minced)
- Arugula – 2 Cups
- Freshly Squeezed Lemon Juice – ¼ Cup

Procedure:

1. In a large bowl, add all of the listed ingredients
2. Mix well to combine.
3. Cover and refrigerate for at least 2 hours or overnight.
4. Serve and enjoy!

Storage: It can be stored in airtight BPA Safe containers for around 4-5 days in the refrigerator and 4-6 months in the freezer.

Nutrition value per serving: Calories: 528 kcal, Fat: 2 g, Carbs: 10 g, Protein: 2 g, Sugar: 200 mg, Potassium: 100 mg

15 FISH AND SHELLFISH RECIPES

15.1 Pesto And Lemon Halibut

Preparation Time: 10 minutes
Cooking Time: 10 minutes
Servings: 4
Ingredients:

- Lemon Juice – 1 Tbsp.
- Lemon Rind, – 1 Tbsp.
- Garlic– 2 Cloves (Peeled)
- Olive Oil – 2 Tbsp.
- Parmesan Cheese– ¼ Cup
- Firmly Packed Basil Leaves – 2/3 Cup
- Freshly Ground Black Pepper – 1/8 Tsp.
- Salt – ¼ Tsp.
- Halibut Fillets - 4 Whole (5 Oz. Each)
- Pesto – 1 cup
- Onion – 1 whole (Diced)

Procedure:

1. In a medium bowl, combine the pesto, lemon juice, salt, and pepper. Reserve 1 tablespoon of the pesto mixture for brushing on the halibut.
2. Heat the olive oil in a large skillet over medium heat. Add the halibut and cook until browned on both sides, about 3 minutes per side. Remove from the skillet and set aside.
3. Add the onion to the skillet and cook until softened, about 5 minutes. Add the garlic and cook for 1 minute longer.
4. Add the reserved pesto mixture to the skillet and bring it to a boil. Cook for 2 minutes longer to blend the flavors. Return the halibut to the skillet and spoon some of the sauce over each fillet. Serve immediately.
5. Garnish with basil if needed

Storage: It can be stored in airtight, BPA Safe containers for up to 2-4 days on average in the fridge. If you prefer to store it in the freezer, you can go up to 4-6 months on average. However, a dish containing Shrimp, Crayfish, and Squid can be stored in the freezer for up to 18 months.

Nutrition value per serving: Calories: 528 kcal, Fat: 2 g, Carbs: 10 g, Protein: 2 g, Sugar: 245 mg, Potassium: 200 mg

15.2 Pecan Crusted Trout

Preparation Time: 10 minutes
Cooking Time: 12 minute
Servings: 4
Ingredients:

- Crushed Pecans – ½ Cup
- Fresh Ginger – ½ Tsp. (Grated)
- 1 Egg,– 1 Whole (Beaten)
- Dried Rosemary – 1 Tsp. (Crushed)
- Salt -1 Tsp.
- Trout Fillets – 4 Whole (4 Oz. Each)
- Black Pepper– As Needed
- Cooking Oil – As Needed
- Whole Wheat Flour- As Needed

Procedure:

1. Grease baking sheet lightly with cooking spray and preheat oven to 400oF.
2. In a shallow bowl, combine black pepper, salt, rosemary, and pecans. In another shallow bowl, add whole wheat flour. In a third bowl, add beaten egg.
3. To prepare fish, dip in flour until covered well. Shake off excess flour. Then dip into beaten egg until coated well. Let excess egg drip off before dipping trout fillet into pecan crumbs. Press the trout lightly onto pecan crumbs to make it stick to the fish.
4. Place breaded fish onto prepared pan. Repeat the process for the remaining fillets.
5. Pop into the oven and bake for 10 to 12 minutes or until fish is flaky.

Storage: It can be stored in airtight, BPA Safe containers for up to 2-4 days on average in the fridge. If you prefer to store it in the freezer, you can go up to 4-6 months on average. However, a dish containing Shrimp, Crayfish, and Squid can be stored in the freezer for up to 18 months.

Nutrition value per serving: Calories: 528 kcal, Fat: 2 g, Carbs: 10 g, Protein: 2 g, Sugar: 245 mg, Potassium: 200 mg

15.3 Spicy Paprika And Salmon Green Beans

Preparation Time: 10 minutes
Cooking Time: 20 minutes
Servings: 4
Ingredients:

- Olive Oil – ¼ Cup
- Cayenne Pepper – ½ Tsp.
- Smoked Paprika – 1 Tbsp.
- Green Beans – 1 Lb.
- Minced Garlic – 2 Tsp. (Minced)
- Fresh Herbs – 3 Tbsp.
- Salmon Steak - 5 Oz.
- Salt And Pepper To Taste - As Needed
- Tomato – 1 Whole (Diced)
- Chili Power – 1 tsp.
- Vinegar – 1 tsp.
- Vegetable Broth – 1 Cup

Procedure:

1. In a large skillet over medium heat, sauté onion and garlic in olive oil until softened. Add the salmon, tomatoes, smoked paprika, green beans, cayenne, chili powder, salt, and black pepper;
2. Bring to a boil. Reduce heat and simmer for 10 minutes.
3. In a small bowl, whisk together the broth and vinegar. Pour into the skillet; bring to a boil. Cook for 3 minutes or until the sauce is slightly thickened. Sprinkle with parsley and rosemary before serving.

Storage: It can be stored in airtight, BPA Safe containers for up to 2-4 days on average in the fridge. If you prefer to store it in the freezer, you can go up to 4-6 months on average. However, a dish containing Shrimp, Crayfish, and Squid can be stored in the freezer for up to 18 months.

Storage: It can be stored in airtight, BPA Safe containers for up to 2-4 days on average in the fridge. If you prefer to store it in the freezer, you can go up to 4-6 months on average. However, a dish containing Shrimp, Crayfish, and Squid can be stored in the freezer for up to 18 months.

Nutrition value per serving: Calories: 528 kcal, Fat: 2 g, Carbs: 10 g, Protein: 2 g, Sugar: 245 mg, Potassium: 200 mg

15.4 Pan Fried Tuna And Herbs Meal

Preparation Time: 10 minutes
Cooking Time: 5 minutes
Servings: 4
Ingredients:

- Almonds– ¼ Cup (Chopped)
- Tangerine Juice – ¼ Cup
- Fennel Seeds– ½ Tsp.
- Ground Pepper– ½ Tsp.
- Sea Salt – ½ Tsp.
- Olive Oil – 1 Tbsp.
- Fresh Mint– 2 Tbsp. (Chopped)
- Red Onion– 2 Tbsp. (Chopped)
- Tuna Steak - 4 Whole (5 Oz. Each, Cut Int Half)

Procedure:

1. Mix fennel seeds, olive oil, mint, onion, tangerine juice, and almonds in a small bowl. Season with ¼ tsp. each of pepper and salt.
2. Season fish with the remaining pepper and salt.
3. On medium-high fire, place a large nonstick fry pan and grease with cooking spray.
4. Pan fry tuna until the desired doneness is reached or for one minute per side.
5. Transfer cooked tuna to a serving plate, drizzle with dressing and serve.

Storage: It can be stored in airtight, BPA Safe containers for up to 2-4 days on average in the fridge. If you prefer to store it in the freezer, you can go up to 4-6 months on average. However, a dish containing Shrimp, Crayfish, and Squid can be stored in the freezer for up to 18 months.

Nutrition value per serving: Calories: 528 kcal, Fat: 2 g, Carbs: 10 g, Protein: 2 g, Sugar: 245 mg, Potassium: 200 mg

15.5 Orange And Herbed Sauce White Bass

Preparation Time: 10 minutes
Cooking Time: 33 minutes
Servings: 4
Ingredients:

- Onions – ¼ Cup (Sliced)
- Orange Juice – ½ Cup
- Fresh Lemon Juice – 1 And ½ Tbsp.
- Olive Oil – 1 And ½ Tbsp.
- Onion– 1 Large Sized (Halved)
- Orange– 1 Large (Unpeeled And Sliced)
- Fresh – 3 Tbsp. (Chopped)
- Skinless White Bass Fillets – 5 Whole (3 Oz. Each, Skinless)
- Additional Unpeeled Orange Slices – As Needed
- Salt and Pepper – As Needed
- Thyme And Oregano – 1 tsp. each

Procedure:

1. Preheat the oven to 400 °F.
2. Season white bass with olive oil, salt, and pepper. Place on a baking sheet and roast in preheated oven for 10 minutes.
3. In a small bowl, mix together orange segments, parsley, thyme, and oregano.
4. To prepare sauce, mix the orange mixture with reserved pan juices from the fish.
5. Serve over grilled white bass.

Storage: It can be stored in airtight, BPA Safe containers for up to 2-4 days on average in the fridge. If you prefer to store it in the freezer, you can go up to 4-6 months on average. However, a dish containing Shrimp, Crayfish, and Squid can be stored in the freezer for up to 18 months.

Nutrition value per serving: Calories: 528 kcal, Fat: 2 g, Carbs: 10 g, Protein: 2 g, Sugar: 245 mg, Potassium: 200 mg

15.6 One-Pot Seafood Chowder

Preparation Time: 10 minutes
Cooking Time: 10 minutes
Servings: 4
Ingredients:

- Coconut Milk – 3 Cups
- Garlic – 1 Tbsp. (Minced)
- Salt And Pepper – As Needed
- Clams – 3 Cups (Chopped)
- Shrimps – 2 Cups
- Fresh Shrimps,1 Pack (Shelled And Deveined)
- Corn, – 1 Cup (Drained)
- Potatoes – 4 (Large Sized, Diced)
- Carrots– 2 Whole (Peeled And Chopped)
- Celery Stalks- 2 Whole (Chopped)
- Onions – ½ cup (Sliced)
- Bell Pepper – 1 Whole (Sliced)

Procedure:

1. In a large pot or Dutch oven, sauté onions and peppers in olive oil over medium heat until softened.
2. Add garlic and sauté for an additional minute. Stir in remaining ingredients except for shrimp to the pot and bring the mix to a boil
3. Reduce heat to low and simmer for 30 minutes.
4. Add shrimp and simmer for an additional 5 minutes or until shrimp turn pink. Season with salt and black pepper to taste.
5. Serve hot.

Storage: It can be stored in airtight, BPA Safe containers for up to 2-4 days on average in the fridge. If you prefer to store it in the freezer, you can go up to 4-6 months on average. However, a dish containing Shrimp, Crayfish, and Squid can be stored in the freezer for up to 18 months.

Nutrition value per serving: Calories: 528 kcal, Fat: 2 g, Carbs: 10 g, Protein: 2 g, Sugar: 245 mg, Potassium: 200 mg

15.7 Lemon And Garlic Baked Halibut

Preparation Time: 10 minutes
Cooking Time: 15 minutes
Servings: 4

Ingredients:

- Garlic Clove,- 1 Clove (Minced)
- Flat Leaf Parsley – 1 Tbsp. (Chopped)
- Olive Oil – 1 Tsp.
- Halibut Fillets – 2 Fillets (5 Oz. Each, Skin On)
- Lemon Zest – 2 Tsp.
- Lemon, Divided – ½ A Lemon
- Salt And Pepper - As Needed
- Honey – 1 Tsp.
- Lemon Juice – 1 Tsp.
- Tomato -1 Whole (Diced)

Procedure:

1. Place the halibut fillets in the dish and drizzle with olive oil. Sprinkle with lemon juice, honey, garlic, salt, and pepper.
2. Bake for about 20 minutes or until fish flakes easily when tested with a fork.
3. Remove from oven and sprinkle with tomatoes, parsley leaves, and any additional seasoning desired. Serve hot.

Storage: It can be stored in airtight, BPA Safe containers for up to 2-4 days on average in the fridge. If you prefer to store it in the freezer, you can go up to 4-6 months on average. However, a dish containing Shrimp, Crayfish, and Squid can be stored in the freezer for up to 18 months.

Nutrition value per serving: Calories: 528 kcal, Fat: 2 g, Carbs: 10 g, Protein: 2 g, Sugar: 245 mg, Potassium: 200 mg

15.8 Poached Trout Meal

Preparation Time: 10 minutes
Cooking Time: 10 minutes
Servings: 4

Ingredients:

- Lemon Juice – 1 Tbsp.
- Leeks, Halved – 2 (Halved)
- Trout Fillet – 1 Whole (8 Oz. , Boneless And Skin On)
- Chicken Broth Or Water – 2 Cups
- Salt And Pepper - As Needed
- Onion – 1 Whole (Sliced)
- Garlic – 1 Whole (Cloves, Sliced)
- For Garnish – Raisin, Pine Nuts etc.

Procedure:

1. In a large skillet or wok, heat the oil over high heat. Add the trout and cook for 1 minute per side or until browned. Remove from the pan and set aside.
2. In the same pan, add the leeks, onion, and garlic and stir fry for 2 minutes. Add the chicken broth and lemon juice and bring to a boil.
3. Lower the heat and simmer for 10 minutes or until the vegetables are tender.
4. Season with salt and pepper to taste.
5. Spoon the vegetables over the trout in the skillet and sprinkle with parsley, pine nuts, raisins, and any other desired garnishes. Serve immediately.

Storage: It can be stored in airtight, BPA Safe containers for up to 2-4 days on average in the fridge. If you prefer to store it in the freezer, you can go up to 4-6 months on average. However, a dish containing Shrimp, Crayfish, and Squid can be stored in the freezer for up to 18 months.

Nutrition value per serving: Calories: 528 kcal, Fat: 2 g, Carbs: 10 g, Protein: 2 g, Sugar: 245 mg, Potassium: 200 mg

15.9 Salmon And Corn Pepper Salsa

Preparation Time: 10 minutes
Cooking Time: 10-12 minute
Servings: 4

Ingredients:

For Spicy Salmon

- Garlic Clove – 1 Clove
- Mild Chili Powder – ½ Tsp.
- Ground Coriander – ½ Tsp.
- Ground Cumin – ¼ Tsp.
- Grated Zest – 1 Lime (Grated)
- Rapeseed Oil – 2 Tsp.
- Salmon Fillets – 2 Whole

For Salsa Salad

- Corn On The Cob– 1 Whole (Husk Removed)
- Red Pepper – 1 Whole (Deseeded And Chopped)
- Red Chili – 1 Whole (Halved)
- Coriander – ½ A Pack (Chopped)
- Lime Juice – 1 Tbsp.
- Lime Wedges – As Needed
- Salsa- As Needed For Serving

Procedure:

1. Take a bowl and grate up the garlic
2. Boil the corn for about 6-8 minutes until they are tender
3. Drain off and cut off the kernels
4. Take your garlic bowl and add the spices, 1 tablespoon of lime juice, and oil
5. Mix well to prepare a spice rub
6. Coat the salmon with the rub
7. Add the rest of the zest to the corn and give it a nice stir
8. Take a frying pan and place it over medium heat
9. Add salmon and cook for about 2 minutes on each side
10. Serve the cooked salmon with salsa and lime wedges!
11. Enjoy!

Storage: It can be stored in airtight, BPA Safe containers for up to 2-4 days on average in the fridge. If you prefer to store it in the freezer, you can go up to 4-6 months on average. However, a dish containing Shrimp, Crayfish, and Squid can be stored in the freezer for up to 18 months.

Nutrition value per serving: Calories: 530 kcal, Fat: 32 g, Carbs: 27 g, Protein: 29 g, Sugar: 245 mg, Potassium: 200 mg

15.10 Spicy Cajun Shrimp

Preparation Time: 10 minutes
Cooking Time: 50 minute
Servings: 4

Ingredients:

For the Dish

- Garlic – 3 Cloves (Crushed)
- Grass Fed Butter – 3 Tbsp.
- Jumbo Shrimps - 20 Pieces

For The Cajun Seasoning

- Paprika – 1 Tsp.
- Cayenne Pepper – Just A Dash
- Himalayan Sea Salt – ½ Tsp.
- Red Pepper Flakes – Just A Dash
- Garlic Granules – 1 Tsp.
- Onion Powder – 1 Tsp.

For Others

- Zucchinis – 2 Large Sized (Spiralized)
- Red Pepper – 1 Whole (Sliced)
- Onion – 1 Whole (Sliced)
- Grass Fed Butter – 1 Tbsp.
- Cilantro – For Garnish

Procedure:

1. In a large pot or Dutch oven, heat the oil over medium heat.
2. Add the onion and bell pepper and cook until softened, about 5 minutes.
3. Add the garlic and cook for 1 minute longer.
4. Add all the remaining ingredients to the pot and stir well. Bring the mixture to boil, then lower it down to a simmer. Cook for 10 minutes
5. Stir in the cilantro and serve.

Storage: It can be stored in airtight, BPA Safe containers for up to 2-4 days on average in the fridge. If you prefer to store it in the freezer, you can go up to 4-6 months on average. However, a dish containing Shrimp, Crayfish, and Squid can be stored in the freezer for up to 18 months.

Nutrition value per serving: Calories: 92 kcal, Fat: 8 g, Carbs: 2 g, Protein: 5 g, Sugar: 245 mg, Potassium: 200 mg

15.11 Asparagus Salmon Fillets

Preparation Time: 10 minutes
Cooking Time: 10 minute
Servings: 4
Ingredients:

- Salmon Fillets -2 Whole Fillets, 6 Oz Each (Skinless)
- Salt – As Needed
- Asparagus – 1 lb. (Trimmed)
- Garlic – 2 Cloves (Minced)
- Butter – 3 Tbsp.
- Parmesan Cheese – ¼ Cup (Grated)

Procedure:

1. Preheat the oven to 400°F (200°C).
2. Grease a baking sheet with cooking spray or oil.
3. Pat the salmon dry using a paper towel and season with salt as desired.
4. Arrange the salmon fillets in the center of the baking sheet and surround them with the asparagus.
5. In a small saucepan over medium heat, melt the butter.
6. Add the minced garlic and cook for 3 minutes, or until slightly golden.
7. Drizzle the butter-garlic sauce evenly over the salmon and asparagus.
8. Sprinkle the grated parmesan cheese on top of the salmon fillets.
9. Bake for 12 minutes, or until the salmon is cooked through and flakes easily.
10. Serve immediately and enjoy!

Storage: It can be stored in airtight, BPA Safe containers for up to 2-4 days on average in the fridge. If you prefer to store it in the freezer, you can go up to 4-6 months on average. However, a dish containing Shrimp, Crayfish, and Squid can be stored in the freezer for up to 18 months.

Nutrition value per serving: Calories: 250 kcal, Fat: 13 g, Carbs: 10 g, Protein: 27 g, Sugar: 1 g, Potassium: 200 mg

Nutrition value per serving: Calories: 200 kcal, Fat: 12 g, Carbs: 17 g, Protein: 8 g, Sugar: 245 mg, Potassium: 200 mg

15.12 Hearty Glazed Salmon Meal

Preparation Time: 10 minutes
Cooking Time: 15 minute
Servings: 4
Ingredients:

- Salmon Fillets – 4 Pieces (5 Ounce Each)
- Coconut Aminos – 4 Tbsp.
- Olive Oil – 4 Tsp.
- Ginger – 2 Tsp. (Minced)
- Sugar-Free Ketchup – 2 Tbsp.
- Dry White Wine – 4 Tbsp.
- Red Boat Fish Sauce – 2 Tbsp.

Procedure:

1. Take a bowl and mix in coconut aminos, garlic, ginger, fish sauce, and mix
2. Add salmon and let it marinate for 15-20 minutes
3. Take a skillet/pan and place it over medium heat
4. Add oil and let it heat up
5. Add salmon fillets and cook on HIGH for 3-4 minutes per side
6. Remove dish once crispy
7. Add sauce and wine
8. Simmer for 5 minutes on low heat
9. Return salmon to the glaze and flip until both sides are glazed
10. Serve and enjoy!

Storage: It can be stored in airtight, BPA Safe containers for up to 2-4 days on average in the fridge. If you prefer to store it in the freezer, you can go up to 4-6 months on average. However, a dish containing Shrimp, Crayfish, and Squid can be stored in the freezer for up to 18 months.

Nutrition value per serving: Calories: 360 kcal, Fat: 15 g, Carbs: 12 g, Protein: 43 g, Sugar: 245 mg, Potassium: 200 mg

15.13 Traditionally Cooked Salmon

Preparation Time: 10 minutes
Cooking Time: 15 minute
Servings: 4
Ingredients:

- Garlic Cloves – 4 Cloves (Pressed)
- Balsamic Vinegar – ¼ Cup
- Olive Oil – ½ Cup
- Salmon Fillets – 4 Whole
- Salt And Pepper - 1 And ½ Tsp.
- Oregano – 1 tsp.
- Thyme – 1 tsp.
- Parsley – 1 tsp. For Garnish
- Lemon Juice – 1 Tbsp.

Procedure:

1. Preheat the oven to 350 °F (175 degrees C).
2. In a large skillet over medium heat, heat olive oil. Add garlic, oregano, thyme, and black pepper; cook for 1 minute.
3. Place salmon in the skillet; cook for 3 minutes per side or until browned.
4. Remove salmon from skillet; place on a baking sheet. Bake for 10 minutes or until just cooked through.
5. Remove from oven; garnish with lemon juice and parsley leaves. Serve immediately.

Nutrition value per serving: Calories: 400 kcal, Fat: 35 g, Carbs: 3 g, Protein: 15 g, Sugar: 245 mg, Potassium: 200 mg

15.14 Mediterranean Tilapia Delight

Preparation Time: 10 minutes
Cooking Time: 15 minute
Servings: 4
Ingredients:

- Tilapia – 4 fillets
- Lemon Juice – 1 Tbsp.
- Olive Oil – As Needed For Cooking
- Salt And Pepper – As Needed
- Onions - 1 Whole (Sliced)
- Bell Pepper – 1 Whole (Sliced)
- Garlic – 1 Tbsp. (Minced)
- Oregano – 1 Tbsp. (Dried)
- Tomatoes – 1 Whole (Sliced)

Procedure:

1. Preheat the oven to 375°F (190°C). In a large baking dish, place the tilapia fillets in a single layer.
2. In a separate bowl, combine the olive oil, lemon juice, salt, and pepper. Mix well.
3. Drizzle the olive oil mixture over the tilapia fillets, ensuring they are evenly coated.
4. Bake the tilapia in the preheated oven for 15 minutes or until it is cooked through and flakes easily.
5. Meanwhile, in a medium skillet over medium heat, sauté the onions and bell peppers with some olive oil until they become tender.
6. Add the minced garlic and dried oregano, cooking for another minute.
7. Stir in the sliced tomatoes and let the mixture simmer for approximately 10 minutes or until thoroughly heated.

Storage: Keep leftovers in an airtight container in the refrigerator for up to 2-3 days. For longer storage, place the tilapia in a well-sealed container or wrap it tightly, then store it in the freezer for up to 4-6 months.

Nutrition value per serving: Calories: 183 kcal, Fat: 10 g, Carbs: 18 g, Protein: 24 g, Sugar: 4 g, Potassium: 200 mg

16 PASTA RECIPES

16.1 Lebanese Thin Pasta

Preparation Time: 10 minutes
Cooking Time: 25 minutes
Servings: 4

Ingredients:

- Sea Salt – ¼ Tsp.
- Garlic Cloves– 2 Cloves (Mashed)
- Water – ½ Cup
- Extra-Virgin Olive Oil – 1 Tbsp.
- Low-Sodium Vegetable Soup – 2 Cups
- Vermicelli - 3 Oz. (Broken Down To 1 Inch Pieces)
- Cabbage – 3 Cups
- Brown Rice -1 Cup
- Red Pepper Flakes - ½ Tsp. (Crushed)
- Cilantro – ½ Cup (Chopped)
- Fresh Lemon Slices, For Serving – For Serving
- Feta Cheese – 1 cup (Shredded)
- Parsley – For Garnish

Procedure:

1. Cook the pasta according to package instructions. Drain and return it to the pot.
2. In a large skillet over medium heat, heat the olive oil. Add the onion and garlic and cook until softened, about 5 minutes. Add remaining ingredients except cheese, parsley
3. Stir in the cooked pasta and feta cheese. Top with parsley and Parmesan cheese and serve warm.

Storage: It can be stored in the fridge in an airtight BPA-free container for up to 3-4 days. Storing in a freezer is not recommended as it raises the risk of salmonella colonization.

Nutrition value per serving: Calories: 528 kcal, Fat: 2 g, Carbs: 10 g, Protein: 2 g, Sugar: 245 mg, Potassium: 200 mg

16.2 Walnut And Ricotta Spaghetti

Preparation Time: 10 minutes
Cooking Time: 10 minutes
Servings: 4

Ingredients:

- Whole-Wheat Spaghetti – 2 Cups
- Walnuts– ¼ Cup (Toasted, Chopped)
- Sea Salt And Freshly Ground - As Needed
- Ricotta Cheese – 2 Tbsp.
- Pepper, To Taste- As Needed
- Parmesan Cheese – ½ Cup (Grated)
- Garlic– 4 Cloves (Minced)
- Flat-Leaf Parsley– ¼ Cup (Chopped)
- Extra-Virgin Olive Oil - 2 Tbsp.
- Red Onion – 1 Whole (Sliced)
- Thyme – 1 Tsp.
- Sugar – 1 Tbsp.

Procedure:

1. Cook the spaghetti according to the package instructions. Drain well and return it to the pot.
2. While the pasta is cooking, heat the oil in a large skillet over medium heat. Add the walnuts and sauté for 2 minutes, stirring occasionally. Add the red onion and garlic and cook for 5 minutes more, until everything is softened. Add the diced tomatoes, parsley, thyme, sugar, and salt and bring to a simmer. Lower the heat to low and cook for 10 minutes more, until everything is heated through.
3. Meanwhile, mix together the ricotta cheese and feta cheese in a small bowl. Once the sauce has cooked down

Storage: It can be stored in the fridge in an airtight BPA-free container for up to 3-4 days. Storing in a freezer is not recommended as it raises the risk of salmonella colonization.

Nutrition value per serving: Calories: 528 kcal, Fat: 2 g, Carbs: 10 g, Protein: 2 g, Sugar: 245 mg, Potassium: 200 mg

16.3 Butternut Squash And Zucchini Penne

Preparation Time: 10 minutes
Cooking Time: 30 minute
Servings: 4
Ingredients:

- Zucchini– 1 Whole (Diced)
- Whole-Grain Penne – 2 Cups
- Sea Salt – ½ Tsp.
- Parmesan Cheese – 2 Tbsp.
- Freshly Ground Black Pepper – ½ Tsp.
- Extra-Virgin Olive Oil – 1 Tbsp.
- Butternut Squash– 1 Large (Peeled And Diced)
- Marinara Sauce – 1 Cup

Procedure:

1. Preheat oven to 375 °F (190 degrees C).
2. In a large bowl, combine butternut squash and zucchini.
3. Pour marinara sauce over the top and mix well.
4. Spread mixture into an 8x8 inch baking dish.
5. Sprinkle with Parmesan cheese, salt, and pepper.
6. Bake for 30 minutes, or until vegetables are tender.
7. Meanwhile, cook spaghetti in a large pot of boiling water following package instructions.
8. Drain spaghetti and add it to the baking dish with the olive oil and salt and pepper to taste. Mix well and bake for 5 more minutes, or until cheese is melted.

Storage: It can be stored in the fridge in an airtight BPA-free container for up to 3-4 days. Storing in a freezer is not recommended as it raises the risk of salmonella colonization.

Nutrition value per serving: Calories: 528 kcal, Fat: 2 g, Carbs: 10 g, Protein: 2 g, Sugar: 245 mg, Potassium: 200 mg

16.4 Red Chicken And Spaghetti

Preparation Time: 10 minutes
Cooking Time: 42 minutes
Servings: 4
Ingredients:

- Spaghetti – 1 Lb.
- Salt – As Needed
- Chicken Broth – 1 Cup
- Milk – 1 Cup
- White Wine – ½ Cup
- Ground Chicken – 1 And ½ Lb.
- Red Pepper Flakes – ¼ Tsp.
- Tomato Paste – ¼ Cup
- Garlic Cloves – 2 Whole (Crushed)
- Carrot – 1 Whole (Minced)
- Onion – 1 Whole (Minced)
- Bacon – 6 Oz. (Cubed)
- Olive Oil – 2 Tbsp.
- Celery – 1 Cup (diced)

Procedure:

1. Take a pressure cooker and add oil, let it warm up over medium heat
2. Add bacon, fry for 5 minutes until crispy
3. Add celery, garlic, carrot, onion and cook for around 5 minutes until fragrant
4. Add red pepper flakes, tomato paste and cook for 2 minutes more
5. Break your chicken into small pieces and add them to the pot
6. Cook for 10 minutes, making sure to keep stirring until browned
7. Add wine, let it simmer for 2 minutes over low heat
8. Add chicken broth, milk
9. Place the lid on top and lock it, let it pressure cook for 10-15 minutes
10. Let the pressure release naturally, open the lid and add spaghetti
11. Lock the lid once more and let it pressure cook for 5 minutes more
12. Quick release the pressure and check the pasta for doneness, once done, serve and enjoy!

Storage

Cooked paste can be stored in an BPA safe container in the fridge for 2-3 days.

Nutrition value per serving: Calories: 477 kcal, Fat: 20 g, Carbs: 48 g, Protein: 28 g, Sodium: 270 mg, Potassium: 280 mg

16.5 Mushroom And Fettucine Platter

Preparation Time: 10 minutes
Cooking Time: 15 minutes
Servings: 4

Ingredients:

- Whole Wheat Fettuccine – 12 Oz.
- Salt – ½ Tsp.
- Mixed Mushrooms Such As Oyst4er, Cremini Etc. – 4 Cups
- Low Fat Milk – 2 Cups
- Garlic – 1 Tbsp. (Minced)
- Freshly Ground Pepper – ½ Tsp.
- Extra Virgin Olive Oil – 1 Tbsp.
- Dry Sherry - ½ Cup
- Brussels Sprouts – 4 Cups (Sliced)
- Asiago Cheese - 1 Cup (Shredded)
- All-Purpose Flour – 2 Tbsp.

Procedure:

1. Take a large sized pot and cook your pasta in boiling water for about 8-10 minutes
2. Drain the pasta and keep them on the side
3. Take a large sized skillet and place it over medium heat
4. Add oil and heat it up
5. Add mushrooms, Brussels and cook for about 8-10 minutes until the mushroom has released the liquid
6. Add garlic and cook for about 1 minute until fragrant
7. Add sherry, making sure to scrape up any brown bits
8. Bring the mix to a boil and cook for about 1 minute until evaporated
9. Take a bowl and whisk flour and milk
10. Add the mix to your skillet
11. Season with some pepper and salt
12. Cook well for about 2 minutes until the sauce begins to bubble and is thickened
13. Stir in Asiago until it has fully melted
14. Add the sauce to your pasta
15. Give it a nice toss
16. Serve with some more cheese
17. Enjoy!

Storage: It can be stored in the fridge in an airtight BPA-free container for up to 3-4 days. Storing in a freezer is not recommended as it raises the risk of salmonella colonization.

Nutrition value per serving: Calories: 384 kcal, Fat: 10 g, Carbs: 56 g, Protein: 18 g, Sugar: 245 mg, Potassium: 200 mg

16.6 Creamy And Wholesome Shrimp Pasta

Preparation Time: 10 minutes
Cooking Time: 15 minutes
Servings: 4

Ingredients:

- Whole Wheat Spaghetti - 5 Oz.
- Raw Shrimp– 12 Oz.
- Asparagus - 1 Bunch (Sliced)
- Large Bell Pepper – 1 Whole (Sliced)
- Garlic – 3 Cloves (Chopped)
- Kosher Salt – 1 And ¼ Tsp.
- Non-Fat Plain Yogurt – 1 And ½ Cups
- Flat Leaf Parsley – ¼ Cup (Chopped)
- Lemon Juice – 3 Tbsp.
- Extra Virgin Olive Oil – 1 Tbsp.
- Fresh Ground Black Pepper – 12 Tsp.
- Pine Nuts - ¼ Cup (Toasted)

Procedure:

1. Take a large sized pot and bring water to a boil
2. Add your spaghetti and cook them for about 2 minutes less than the directed package instruction
3. Add shrimp, bell pepper, asparagus and cook for about 2- 4 minutes until the shrimp are tender
4. Drain the pasta and the contents well
5. Take a large bowl and mash garlic until a paste forms
6. Whisk in yogurt ,parsley, oil, pepper and lemon juice into the garlic paste
7. Add pasta mix and toss well
8. Serve by sprinkling some pine nuts!
9. Enjoy!

Storage: It can be stored in the fridge in an airtight BPA-free container for up to 3-4 days.

Storing in a freezer is not recommended as it raises the risk of salmonella colonization.

Nutrition value per serving: Calories: 361 kcal, Fat: 6 g, Carbs: 53 g, Protein: 28 g, Sugar: 245 mg, Potassium: 200 mg

16.7 Hot And Enticing Lemon Garlic Sardine Fettucine

Preparation Time: 10 minutes
Cooking Time: 15 minute
Servings: 4
Ingredients:

- Whole Wheat Fettuccine – 8 Oz.
- Extra Virgin Olive Oil – 4 Tbsp.
- Garlic – 4 Cloves (Minced)
- Lemon Juice – ¼ Cup
- Freshly Ground Pepper – 1 Tsp.
- Salt – ½ Tsp.
- Sardines (Dipped In Tomato Sauce) – 8 Oz. (Boneless And Skinless)

Procedure:

1. Cook spaghetti according to package instructions. Drain well.
2. In a large skillet over medium heat, heat olive oil. Add lemon juice, garlic, salt and pepper.
3. Cook until garlic is fragrant.
4. Add sardines and cook until browned. Serve over spaghetti.

Storage: It can be stored in the fridge in an airtight BPA-free container for up to 3-4 days. Storing in a freezer is not recommended as it raises the risk of salmonella colonization.

Nutrition value per serving: Calories: 480 kcal, Fat: 21 g, Carbs: 53 g, Protein: 23 g, Sugar: 245 mg, Potassium: 200 mg

16.8 Tuna And Olive Pasta

Preparation Time: 10 minutes
Cooking Time: 15 minutes
Servings: 4
Ingredients:

- Whole Wheat Gobetti, Rotini Or Penne Pasta - 5 Oz.
- Tuna Steak– 8 Oz. (Cut)
- Garlic – 3 Cloves (Minced)
- Fresh Oregano – 2 Tsp. (Chopped)
- Fresh Ground Pepper – ¼ Tsp.
- Extra Virgin Olive Oil – 4 Tbsp.
- Divided Salt – ½ Tsp.

Procedure:

1. Cook pasta according to package instructions. Drain.
2. In a large skillet over medium heat, heat olive oil. Add tuna, garlic, salt, pepper, oregano, and thyme; cook for about 5 minutes or until tuna is cooked through.
3. Add pasta and parsley; toss to combine. Serve warm.

Storage: It can be stored in the fridge in an airtight BPA-free container for up to 3-4 days. Storing in a freezer is not recommended as it raises the risk of salmonella colonization.

Nutrition value per serving: Calories: 422 kcal, Fat: 17 g, Carbs: 42 g, Protein: 22 g, Sugar: 245 mg, Potassium: 200 mg

16.9 The Perfect Basil Pasta

Preparation Time: 10 minutes
Cooking Time: 15 minutes
Servings: 4

Ingredients:

- Red Pepper Seeded– 2 Whole (Seeded And Cut Into Chunks)
- Red Onion– 2 Whole (Cu Into Wedges)
- Mild Red Chilies – 2 Whole (Diced And Seeded)
- Garlic Cloves – 3 Cloves (Chopped)
- Golden Caster Sugar – 1 Tsp.
- Olive Oil (Plus Additional For Serving) – 2 Tbsp.
- Small Ripe Tomatoes– 2 Lb.
- Dried Pasta – 12 Oz.
- Basil Leaves - Handful
- Parmesan - 2 Tbsp.

Procedure:

1. Pre-heat your oven to a temperature of 392 degree Fahrenheit
2. Take a large sized roasting tin and scatter peppers, red onion, garlic and chilies
3. Sprinkle sugar on top
4. Drizzle olive oil and season with some salt and pepper
5. Roast the veggies for 15 minutes
6. Add tomatoes and roast for another 15 minutes
7. Take a large sized pan and cook your pasta in salted boiling water according to instructions
8. Drain them once ready
9. Remove the veggies from the oven and tip in the pasta carefully
10. Toss everything well
11. Tear the basil leaves on top
12. Sprinkle a bit of parmesan
13. Enjoy!

Storage: It can be stored in the fridge in an airtight BPA-free container for up to 3-4 days. Storing in a freezer is not recommended as it raises the risk of salmonella colonization.

Nutrition value per serving: Calories: 452 kcal, Fat: 8 g, Carbs: 88 g, Protein: 14 g, Sugar: 245 mg, Potassium: 200 mg

16.10 Mediterranean Chicken And Bacon Pasta

Preparation Time: 10 minutes
Cooking Time: 20 minute
Servings: 4

Ingredients:

- Tomatoes With Juice – 4 Oz. (Peeled And Diced)
- Salt As Needed – As Needed
- Linguine Pasta – 8 Oz.
- Feta Cheese – 1/3 Cup (Crumbled)
- Dried Rosemary – ¼ Tsp.
- Chicken Breast Half– 1 Lb. (Cooked Up And Diced)
- Black Olives – 2/3 Cup (Pitted)
- Bacon – 3 Slices
- Artichoke Hearts (6 Ounce) - 5 Oz.

Procedure:

1. Take al large sized pot and fill it up with salted water
2. Bring the water to a boil and add linguine
3. Cook for 8-10 minutes until Al Dente
4. Take a large sized deep skillet and cook the Bacon until brown
5. Crumble the bacon and keep it on the side
6. Season your chicken with salt
7. Stir the chicken and bacon into a large sized skillet
8. Add tomatoes and rosemary and simmer the whole mixture for about 20 minutes
9. Stir in feta cheese, artichokes hearts, olives and cook until thoroughly heated
10. Toss the freshly cooked pasta with the breast and serve immediately!
11. Garnish with some extra feta if your heart desires

Storage: It can be stored in the fridge in an airtight BPA-free container for up to 3-4 days. Storing in a freezer is not recommended as it raises the risk of salmonella colonization.

Nutrition value per serving: Calories: 625 kcal, Fat: 26 g, Carbs: 50 g, Protein: 45 g, Sugar: 245 mg, Potassium: 200 mg

16.11 Veggie Friendly Mediterranean Pasta

Preparation Time: 10 minutes
Cooking Time: 120 minutes
Servings: 4
Ingredients:
For Sauce

- Tomatoes – 28 Oz. (Chopped)
- Sun-Dried Tomato Paste – 1 Tbsp.
- Salt – ½ Tsp.
- Oregano – 1 Tsp.
- Onion – 1 Small (Chopped)
- Olive Oil – 1 Tbsp.
- Garlic (Finely Chopped) – 2 Small Cloves (Chopped)
- Freshly Ground Black Pepper – As Needed
- Dried Thyme – 1 Tsp.
- Dried Parsley – 1 Tsp.
- Dried Basil – 1 Tsp.
- Brown Sugar – ½ Tsp.
- Bay Leaf – 1 Leaf

For Veggies

- Ripened Tomatoes - 12 Small
- Olive Oil – 2 To 3 Tbsp.
- Garlic Cloves – 2 Cloves
- Deseeded Red Peppers – 2 Whole
- Courgettes – 2 Whole
- Aubergine- 1 Whole

For serving

- pasta of your preferred shape such as gigli, conchiglie etc. – 1 lb.
- parmesan cheese -3 and ½ oz.

Procedure:

1. Cook pasta according to package instructions
2. Take a large sized skillet and heat up oil
3. Add the veggies to skillet and Saute for around 5-10 minutes until tender
4. Take another bowl and add the sauce ingredients. Cook for around 5-10 minutes until you have a thick sauce
5. Add the vegetables and pasta to the sauce, stir well
6. Serve and enjoy!

Storage: It can be stored in the fridge in an airtight BPA-free container for up to 3-4 days. Storing in a freezer is not recommended as it raises the risk of salmonella colonization.

Nutrition value per serving: Calories: 252 kcal, Fat: 17 g, Carbs: 20 g, Protein: 0 g, Sugar: 238 mg, Potassium: 243 mg

16.12 Broccoli And Carrot Pasta

Preparation Time: 10 minutes
Cooking Time: 10 minutes
Servings: 4
Ingredients:

- Whole-Wheat Pasta – 8 Oz.
- Sea Salt And Freshly Ground Pepper– As Needed
- Peeled And Shredded Carrots – 1 Cup
- Greek Yogurt – ¼ Cup
- Broccoli Florets – 2 Cups
- Onion – 1 Cup, sliced
- Garlic – 6 Cloves (Diced)
- Fresh Thyme – 1 tsp.

Procedure:

1. Preheat oven to 375 °F (190 degrees C).
2. Cook pasta according to package instructions; drain.
3. Heat oil in large skillet over medium heat. Add onion and garlic; cook until softened, about 5 minutes.
4. Add carrot and broccoli; cook until cabbage is tender, about 10 minutes.
5. Sprinkle with thyme and salt and pepper; add chicken broth and bring to a simmer.
6. Transfer mixture to baking dish; cover with foil and bake for 20 minutes. Uncover and bake for 5 minutes more to firm up the sauce.

Storage: It can be stored in the fridge in an airtight BPA-free container for up to 3-4 days. Storing in a freezer is not recommended as it raises the risk of salmonella colonization.

Nutrition value per serving: Calories: 252 kcal, Fat: 17 g, Carbs: 20 g, Protein: 0 g, Sugar: 238 mg, Potassium: 243 mg

17 RICE RECIPES

17.1 Creamy Millet Dish

Preparation Time: 10 minutes
Cooking Time: 10 minutes
Servings: 4
Ingredients:

- Millet – ½ Cup
- Cream Cheese - 1 Oz.
- Salt – ½ Tsp.
- Hot Water 1 And ½ Cups

Procedure:

1. Mix hot water and millet in the saucepan.
2. Boil it for 8 minutes on low heat.
3. Add cream cheese and salt.
4. Carefully stir the cooked millet.

Nutrition value per serving: Calories: 528 kcal, Fat: 2 g, Carbs: 10 g, Protein: 2 g, Sugar: 245 mg, Potassium: 200 mg

17.2 Perfect Rice Stew

Preparation Time: 10 minutes
Cooking Time: 30 minute
Servings: 4
Ingredients:

- Long Grain Rice – 5 Oz.
- Squid – 4 Oz. (Sliced)
- Jalapeno Pepper – 1 Whole (Sliced)
- Tomatoes – ½ Cup (Chopped)
- Onion – 1 Whole (Diced)
- Chicken Stock – 2 Cups
- Avocado Oil - 1 Tbsp.

Procedure:

1. Roast the onion with avocado oil in the skillet for 3-4 minutes or until the onion is light brown.
2. Add squid, jalapeno pepper, and tomatoes.
3. Cook the ingredients for 7 minutes.
4. Then cook rice with water for 15 minutes.
5. Add cooked rice in the squid mixture, stir, and cook for 3 minutes more.

Storage: It can be stored in the fridge in an airtight BPA-free container for up to 4-5 days. Storing in a freezer is not recommended as it raises the risk of salmonella colonization.

Nutrition value per serving: Calories: 528 kcal, Fat: 2 g, Carbs: 10 g, Protein: 2 g, Sugar: 245 mg, Potassium: 200 mg

17.3 Awesome Rice Rolls

Preparation Time: 10 minutes
Cooking Time: 35 minutes
Servings: 4
Ingredients:

- White Cabbage Leaves – 4 Whole
- Ground Chicken – 4 Oz. (Ground)
- Garlic Powder – ½ Tsp.
- Long Grain Rice – ½ Cup (Cooked)
- Chicken Stock – ½ Cup
- Tomatoes – ½ Cup (Chopped)

Procedure:

1. In the bowl, mix ground chicken, garlic powder, and rice.
2. Then put the rice mixture on every cabbage leaf and roll.
3. Arrange the rice rolls in the saucepan.
4. Add chicken stock and tomatoes and close the lid.
5. Cook the rice rolls for 3-5 minutes on low heat.

Storage: It can be stored in the fridge in an airtight BPA-free container for up to 4-5 days. Storing in a freezer is not recommended as it raises the risk of salmonella colonization.

Nutrition value per serving: Calories: 528 kcal, Fat: 2 g, Carbs: 10 g, Protein: 2 g, Sugar: 245 mg, Potassium: 200 mg

17.4 Seafood Rice Meal

Preparation Time: 10 minutes
Cooking Time: 30 minute
Servings: 4
Ingredients:

- Seafood Mix – ½ Cup
- Long Grain Rice – ½ Cup

- Water – 3 Cups
- Olive Oil – 1 Tbsp.
- Ground Coriander – ½ Tsp.

Procedure:

1. Boil the rice with water for 15-18 minutes or until it soaks all water.
2. Then heat olive oil in the saucepan.
3. Add seafood mix and ground coriander. Cook the ingredients for 10 minutes on low heat.
4. Then add rice, stir well, and cook for 5 minutes more.
5. Serve and enjoy once ready.

Nutrition value per serving: Calories: 528 kcal, Fat: 2 g, Carbs: 10 g, Protein: 2 g, Sugar: 245 mg, Potassium: 200 mg

17.5 Salsa Rice Meal

Preparation Time: 10 minutes
Cooking Time: 15 minutes
Servings: 4

Ingredients:

- Long Grain Rice – 9 Ounces
- Chicken Stock – 4 Cups
- Salsa – 1 Cup
- Avocado Oil - 2 Tbsp.

Procedure:

1. Mix chicken stock and rice in the saucepan.
2. Cook the rice for 15 minutes on medium heat.
3. Then cool it to the room temperature and mix with avocado oil and salsa.
4. Serve and enjoy!

Storage: It can be stored in the fridge in an airtight BPA-free container for up to 4-5 days. Storing in a freezer is not recommended as it raises the risk of salmonella colonization.

Nutrition value per serving: Calories: 528 kcal, Fat: 2 g, Carbs: 10 g, Protein: 2 g, Sugar: 245 mg, Potassium: 200 mg

17.6 Rice And Fish Cakes

Preparation Time: 10 minutes
Cooking Time: 10 minutes
Servings: 4

Ingredients:

- Salmon– 6 Oz. (Shredded)
- Basmati Rice – ¼ Cup (Cooked)
- Cilantro – 1 Tsp. (Dried)
- Chili Flakes – ½ Tsp.
- Organic Canola Oil – 1 Tbsp.
- Egg – 1 Whole (Beaten)

Procedure:

1. Mix salmon with egg, basmati rice, dried cilantro, and chili flakes.
2. Heat the organic canola oil in the skillet.
3. Make the small cakes from the salmon mixture and put in the hot oil.
4. Roast the cakes for 2 minutes per side or until they are light brown.

Storage: It can be stored in the fridge in an airtight BPA-free container for up to 4-5 days. Storing in a freezer is not recommended as it raises the risk of salmonella colonization.

Nutrition value per serving: Calories: 528 kcal, Fat: 2 g, Carbs: 10 g, Protein: 2 g, Sugar: 245 mg, Potassium: 200 mg

17.7 Rice And Prunes

Preparation Time: 10 minutes
Cooking Time: 20 minutes
Servings: 4

Ingredients:

- Basmati Rice – 1 And ½ Cups
- Organic Canola Oil – 3 Tbsp.
- Prunes – 5 Whole (Chopped)
- Cream Cheese – ¼ Cup
- Cups Water – 3 And ½ Cups
- Salt - ½ Tsp.

Procedure:

1. Mix water and basmati rice in the saucepan and boil for 15 minutes on low heat.
2. Then add cream cheese, salt, and prunes.
3. Stir the rice carefully and bring it to boil.
4. Add organic canola oil and cook for 1 minute more.

Storage: It can be stored in the fridge in an airtight BPA-free container for up to 4-5 days.

Storing in a freezer is not recommended as it raises the risk of salmonella colonization.

Nutrition value per serving: Calories: 528 kcal, Fat: 2 g, Carbs: 10 g, Protein: 2 g, Sugar: 245 mg, Potassium: 200 mg

18 PIZZA RECIPES

18.1 Fried Cauliflower Pizza

Preparation Time: 10 minutes
Cooking Time: 25-30 minute
Servings: 4
Ingredients:

- Extra-Virgin Olive Oil – 1 Tbsp. + 1 tsp.
- Salt – ¼ Tsp.
- Cauliflower – 1 Medium Sized Head (Cut Into Small Florets)
- Lemon – 1 Large Sized
- Sun-Dried Tomatoes – 6 Whole (Chopped)
- Olives – 1/3 Cup (Pitted And Sliced)
- Egg – 1 Whole (Lightly Beaten)
- Mozzarella Cheese – 1 Cup (Shredded And Partly Skimmed)
- Oregano – ½ Tsp (Dried)
- Freshly Ground Pepper – 1 Tsp.
- Fresh Basil – ¼ Cup (Chopped)

Procedure:

1. Preheat the oven to 450°F (232°C) and line a pizza pan with parchment paper.
2. In a food processor, pulse the cauliflower florets until they resemble rice-sized crumbles.
3. Transfer the cauliflower to a large non-stick skillet over medium heat, then add 1 tablespoon of oil and salt.
4. Cook the cauliflower for 8-10 minutes until it becomes soft, then transfer it to a large bowl and let it cool for 10 minutes.
5. Carefully remove the white pith from the lemon using a sharp knife and discard it.
6. Cut the lemon segments from the membranes, allowing them to fall into a bowl; remove any seeds as needed and drain the juice.
7. Add the chopped sun-dried tomatoes and sliced olives to the lemon segments and toss to combine.
8. Mix the lightly beaten egg, oregano, and shredded cheese into the cooled cauliflower.
9. Spread the mixture onto the prepared baking sheet and shape it into a 10-inch round pizza crust.
10. Drizzle 1 teaspoon of oil evenly over the crust.
11. Bake the pizza for 10-14 minutes, then scatter the lemon-olive mixture on top.
12. Season with some pepper and bake for an additional 8-14 minutes, or until the crust is nicely browned.
13. Garnish the pizza with chopped fresh basil, slice into wedges, and enjoy!

Storage: It can be stored in air-tight containers for 3-4 days in the refrigerator and 1-2 months in the freezer.

Nutrition value per serving: Calories: 356 kcal, Fat: 10 g, Carbs: 12 g, Protein: 10 g, Sodium: 250 mg

18.2 Hearty Chicken And Olives Pizza

Preparation Time: 10 minutes
Cooking Time: 0 minute
Servings: 4
Ingredients:
For Pizza Dough

- All-Purpose Flour – 4 And ½ Cups
- Kosher Salt – 1 And ¾ Tsp.
- Sugar – 1 Tsp.
- Instant Yeast – 1 Tsp.

- Olive Oil – ¼ Cup
- Ice Cold Water – 1 And 13/4 Cups

For Pizza

- Olive Oil – 2 Tbsp.
- Mozzarella Cheese – ¾ Cup (Shredded)
- Rotisserie Chicken – ½ Cup (Chopped)
- Roasted Red Bell Pepper – ¼ Cup (Sliced)
- Assorted Olives – 9 (Sliced)
- Tomato– 1 Whole (Sliced Into Thin Wedges)
- Sliced Sun Dried Tomatoes – ¼ Cup (Sliced)
- Artichokes– ½ Cup (Cut Into Thin Wedges)
- Spinach – ½ Cup
- Feta – ½ Cup (Crumbled)
- Fresh Oregano – 2 Tbsp. (Chopped)
- Fresh Basil – 2 Tbsp (Chopped)
- Roasted Garlic – 10-12 Cloves

Procedure:

1. Prepare the pizza dough by taking a mixer with hook attachment and mixing flour, sugar, salt and yeast
2. Slowly blend it and keep mixing olive oil until fully combined
3. Drizzle some cold water
4. Once combined well, turn the speed to medium and mix for another 5-7 minutes
5. Once done, transfer the flour to a dusted surface and form small sized balls
6. Place the balls on a flour dusted pan (lined up with parchment paper)
7. Pour a bit of olive oil on top of each of the balls
8. Wrap the pan with foil and allow it to chill overnight
9. Roll out the dough once done on a flour dusted surface using your hands and knuckles
10. Once the dough is rolled out, brush more olives
11. Spread the mozzarella cheese on top followed by the vegetables, chicken and chopped up herbs
12. Transfer it to a sheet pan or pizza stone and dust with corn meal
13. Bake at 500 degree Fahrenheit in your oven for about 8-12 minutes
14. Once done, top with some more fresh herbs
15. Enjoy by cutting it up into slices!

Storage: It can be stored in air-tight containers for 3-4 days in the refrigerator and 1-2 months in the freezer.

Nutrition value per serving: Calories: 253 kcal, Fat: 10 g, Carbs: 14 g, Protein: 10 g, Sodium: 300 mg

18.3 Fresh Pesto Pizza

reparation Time: 10 minutes
Cooking Time: 0 minute
Servings: 4
Ingredients:
For Pesto

- Extra Virgin Olive Oil – 1 Cup
- Whole Blanched Toasted Almonds – ½ Cup
- Brined Capers – 2 Tbsp.
- Garlic – 3 Cloves
- Firmly Packed Fresh Basil Leaves – 1 Cup
- Firmly Packed Fresh Oregano Leaves – ½ Cup
- Feta Cheese – 4 Oz. (Crumbled)
- Kalamata Olives - 1 Oz. (Chopped)
- Fresh Lemon Juice – 1 Tbsp.
- Black Pepper – 1 Tsp.
- Freshly Packed Fresh Flat Parsley Leaves – ½ Cup

For Pizza

- Inch Greek Pita Flatbreads – 2 Whole (6 Inches)
- Mozzarella Cheese – ½ Cup
- Tomatoes – 2 Small (Chopped)
- Kalamata Olives – 8 Whole (Pitted)
- Onion – 1 Whole (Sliced)
- Parsley – For Garnish

Procedure:

1. Preheat oven to 350 °F (175 degrees C).

2. Take a bowl and mix the ingredients listed under pesto using an immersion blender to make the pesto sauce
3. Spread pesto over pizza crust.
4. Add mozzarella cheese, tomatoes, parsley and onion.
5. Bake in preheated oven for 20 minutes or until cheese is melted and bubbly.

Storage: It can be stored in air-tight containers for 3-4 days in the refrigerator and 1-2 months in the freezer.

Nutrition value per serving: Calories: 440 kcal, Fat: 20 g, Carbs: 15 g, Protein: 20 g, Sodium: 254 mg

19 BRUSCHETTA RECIPES

19.1 Avocado And Chimichurri Bruschetta

Preparation Time: 10 minutes
Cooking Time: 0 minute
Servings: 4

Ingredients:

- Whole Grain Ciabatta Bread – 6 Whole Pieces (1/2 Inch Thick, Toasted)
- Salt – ¾ Tsp.
- Red Wine Vinegar – 2 Tbsp.
- Red Pepper Flakes – ½ Tsp.
- Olive Oil – ¼ Cup
- Lemon Juice – 2 Tbsp.
- Garlic – 3 Cloves (Minced)
- Fresh Parsley – ¼ Cup (Chopped)
- Dried Oregano – ½ Tsp.
- Cilantro – ¼ Cup (Chopped)
- Black Pepper – ¼ Tsp.
- Avocado – 2 Whole Pieces (Pitted And Cubed)

Procedure:

1. Take a bowl and add lemon juice, garlic, vinegar, salt, and pepper flakes
2. Mix and add oregano and black pepper
3. Whisk in oil and stir in the cilantro and parsley
4. Fold in avocado cubes
5. Toss well
6. Spoon the whole mixture onto toasted bread slices and enjoy!

Storage: It can be stored in the fridge for 3-4 days. Not suitable for long-term storage in the freezer.

Nutrition value per serving: Calories: 247 kcal, Fat: 17 g, Carbs: 20 g, Protein: 5 g, Sodium: 245 mg

19.2 Tomato Bruschetta

Preparation Time: 10 minutes
Cooking Time: 10 minutes
Servings: 4

Ingredients:

- Olive Oil – 1 Tsp.
- Baguette – 1 Whole (Sliced)
- Tomatoes – 6 Whole (Cubed)
- Salt And Black Pepper – Just A Pinch
- Store bought/home made pesto sauce – 1 cup
- Mozzarella cheese – 1 cup (Shredded)
- Parsley – as needed (chopped)

Procedure:

1. Preheat the oven to 350 °F (175 degrees C).
2. On a baking sheet, spread out the sliced Italian bread (baguette) .
3. Spread pesto over the top of the bread slices.

4. Arrange the diced tomatoes over the top of the pesto.
5. Sprinkle shredded mozzarella cheese and chopped parsley over the tomatoes.
6. Bake in the preheated oven for 10-15 minutes, until the cheese is melted and bubbly and the bread is golden brown on top.

Storage: It can be stored in the fridge for 3-4 days. Not suitable for long-term storage in the freezer.

Nutrition value per serving: Calories: 528 kcal, Fat: 2 g, Carbs: 10 g, Protein: 2 g, Sodium: 245 mg

19.3 Chicken Bruschetta Burgers

Preparation Time: 10 minutes

Cooking Time: 16 minutes

Servings: 4

Ingredients:

- Sun-Dried Tomatoes Packed In Olive Oil - 2 Tbsp. (Minced)
- Salt and pepper – ¼ Tsp. each
- Onion – 2 Tbsp. (Minced)
- Olive Oil – 1 Tbsp.
- Mozzarella Balls, Minced – 2 Whole Small Sized (Minced)
- Chicken Breast - 8 Oz. (Ground)
- Basil – 1 Tsp. (Dried)
- Bread crumbs – ½ cup
- Fresh parsley – 1 tsp.
- Fresh thyme – 1 tsp.
- Fresh rosemary – 1 tsp.

Procedure:

1. Preheat oven to 400 °F (200 degrees C). Grease a baking sheet.
2. In a bowl, combine ground chicken, bread crumbs, parsley, rosemary, thyme and pepper. Mix well.
3. Shape mixture into 8 burgers. Heat olive oil in a large skillet over medium heat. Add burgers and cook until browned on both sides, about 3 minutes per side.
4. Place burgers on the prepared baking sheet and bake for 10 minutes. Sprinkle with minced cheese and tomato slices and serve on buns.

Storage: It can be stored in the fridge for 3-4 days. Not suitable for long-term storage in the freezer.

Nutrition value per serving: Calories: 528 kcal, Fat: 2 g, Carbs: 10 g, Protein: 2 g, Sodium: 245 mg

20 SIDES AND SMALL PLATES RECIPES

20.1 Excellent Tuna Croquettes

Preparation Time: 40 minutes + 4 Hours Chill Time

Cooking Time: 25 minutes

Servings: 12

Ingredients:

- Extra-Virgin Olive Oil – 6 Tbsp.
- Heavy Cream – 1 And ¼ Cups
- Red Onion – 1 Tbsp. (Chopped)
- Almond Flour – 5 Tbsp.
- Yellow Fin Tuna – 4 Oz.
- Dried Dill – ½ Tsp.
- Panko Breadcrumbs – 1 Cup
- Capers – 2 Tsp. Minced
- Eggs – 2 (Whole)
- Fresh Black Pepper – ¼ Tsp.

Procedure:

1. Take a large sized skillet and add 6 tbsp of oil, let the oil heat up over medium-low heat
2. Add 5 tbsp of almond flour, cook gently for 2-3 minutes until you have a thin paste and the flour browns slightly
3. Increase heat to medium-high and gently add the heavy cream, carefully whisking for 5 minutes as you keep on adding
4. Remove the heat and stir in tuna, capers, red onion, dill and pepper
5. Pour the mixture into a 8 inch square baking dish (Coated with olive oil), let it cool down to room temperature
6. Cover the mix and let it chill for 4 hours
7. Take 3 separate bowls, in one bowl add eggs (Beaten). In another, add remaining almond flour while in the third add panko
8. Line a baking sheet with parchment
9. Add 1 tbsp of cold dough into flour mix, roll well. Shake off any excess and use your hand to form oval shape
10. Dip the croquette into eggs, and then in panko
11. Place it on the baking sheet, repeat with remaining dough
12. Take a small sized saucepan and add 1-2 cups of olive oil over medium high heat
13. Once the oil is hot, add croquettes and fry them until golden brown

Storage

Since this is a fried item, it is ideal that you consume it right away. However, you may still store it in fridge for 1-2 days in an air tight box, but the taste will deteriorate.

Nutrition value per serving: Calories: 92 kcal, Fat: 5 g, Carbs: 10 g, Protein: 10 g, Sodium: 300 mg, Potassium: 230 mg

20.2 Fancy Wrapped Plums

Preparation Time: 10 minutes

Cooking Time: 0 minute

Servings: 4

Ingredients:

- Prosciutto – 2 Oz. (Cut Into 16 Pieces)
- Plums, – 4 Whole (Quartered)
- Chives – 1 Tbsp. (Chopped)
- Red Pepper Flakes - Just A Pinch (Crushed)
- Salt And Pepper – As Needed

Procedure:

1. Preheat oven to 400 °F (200 degrees C).
2. Cut prosciutto into small pieces.
3. Mix prosciutto, salt, and pepper in a Bowl.
4. Place plums on a baking sheet lined with foil and top with prosciutto mixture.
5. Bake for 30 minutes or until plum is soft.
6. Serve and enjoy!

Storage: It can be stored in BPA Free container for around 4-5 days in the refrigerator. Storage in the Freezer is not recommended

Nutrition value per serving: Calories: 528 kcal, Fat: 2 g, Carbs: 10 g, Protein: 2 g, Sugar: 245 mg, Potassium: 200 mg

20.3 Simple Cheese Mug

Preparation Time: 10 minutes
Cooking Time: 2-5 minute
Servings: 4

Ingredients:

- 2 ounces roast beef slices
- 1 and ½ tablespoons green chilies, diced
- 1 and ½ ounces pepper jack cheese, shredded
- 1 tablespoon sour cream

Procedure:

1. Layer roast beef on the bottom of your mug, making sure to break it down into small pieces
2. Add half a tablespoon of sour cream, add half tablespoon green Chile and half an ounce of pepper jack cheese
3. Keep layering until all ingredients are used
4. Microwave for 2 minutes
5. Server warm and enjoy!

Storage: It can be stored in BPA Free container for around 4-5 days in the refrigerator. Storage in the Freezer is not recommended.

Nutrition value per serving: Calories: 5 kcal, Fat: 2 g, Carbs: 10 g, Protein: 2 g, Sugar: 245 mg, Potassium: 200 mg

20.4 Stuffed Avocado Meal

Preparation Time: 10 minutes
Cooking Time: 0 minute
Servings: 4

Ingredients:

- Basil– 1 Tbsp (Chopped)
- Pine Nuts– 2 Tsp. (Toasted And Chopped)
- Salt And Black Pepper– To Taste
- Black Olives– 2 Tbsp. (Chopped And Pitted)
- Basil Pesto – 1 And ½ Tbsp.
- Sun-Dried Tomatoes – 2 Tbsp. (Chopped)
- Tuna– 10 Oz. (Drained)
- Avocado– 1 Whole (Halved And Pitted)

Procedure:

1. Cut the avocados in half and remove the pit. Scoop out the flesh and place it in a bowl.
2. Into the bowl, add remaining ingredients and mix them thoroughly
3. Stuff the avocados with the mixture and serve immediately.

Storage: It can be stored in BPA Free container for around 4-5 days in the refrigerator. Storage in the Freezer is not recommended.

Nutrition value per serving: Calories: 528 kcal, Fat: 2 g, Carbs: 10 g, Protein: 2 g, Sugar: 245 mg, Potassium: 200 mg

20.5 Yogurt And Banana Bowls

Preparation Time: 10 minutes
Cooking Time: 10 minute
Servings: 4

Ingredients:

- Bananas– 2 Whole (Sliced)
- Nutmeg – ½ Tsp. (Ground)
- Flaxseed Meal – 3 Tbsp.
- Creamy Peanut Butter – ¼ Cup
- Greek Yogurt – 4 Cups

Procedure:

1. Divide Greek yogurt between 4 serving bowls and top with sliced bananas.
2. Add peanut butter in microwave-safe bowl and micro- wave for 30 seconds.
3. Drizzle 1 tbsp. of melted peanut butter on each bowl on top of the sliced bananas.
4. Sprinkle cinnamon and flax meal on top and serve.

Storage: It can be stored in BPA Free container for around 4-5 days in the refrigerator. Storage in the Freezer is not recommended.

Nutrition value per serving: Calories: 528 kcal, Fat: 2 g, Carbs: 10 g, Protein: 2 g, Sugar: 245 mg, Potassium: 200 mg

20.6 Quick Cashew Energy Bites

Preparation Time: 10 minutes + 1 Hour Chill Time
Cooking Time: 0 minute
Servings: 4

Ingredients:

- Cashew Nuts – 2 Cups
- Cinnamon – ¼ Tsp.
- Lemon Zest – 1 Tsp.
- Dates – 4 Tbsp. (Chopped)
- Unsweetened Coconut – 1/3 Cup (Shredded)
- Dried Apricots – ¾ Cups

Procedure:

1. Preheat oven to 350 °F (175 degrees C).
2. Spread cashews in a single layer on a baking sheet and roast for 8 minutes, or until lightly browned.
3. When cashews are done roasting, let cool for 5 minutes.
4. Take a medium bowl add cashew, cinnamon, lemon zest, dates, shredded coconut and apricots. Toss them well and enjoy!

Storage: It can be stored in a BPA Free container for around 7-12 days in the refrigerator and 8-12 months in the freezer.

Nutrition value per serving: Calories: 528 kcal, Fat: 2 g, Carbs: 10 g, Protein: 2 g, Sugar: 245 mg, Potassium: 200 mg

20.7 Chia Almond Butter Pudding

Preparation Time: 10 minutes
Cooking Time: 5 minutes
Servings: 4

Ingredients:

- Chia Seeds – ¼ Cup
- Unsweetened Almond Milk – 1 Cup
- Maple Syrup – 1 And ½ Tbsp.
- Almond Butter - 2 And ½ Tbsp.
- Cinnamon – 1 tsp.
- Applesauce – ½ cup
- Salt – as needed
- Coconut oil – 1 tbsp.
- Sugar - 1 cup
- Plain Flour – ½ cup

Procedure:

1. Preheat oven to 375 °F (190 degrees C). Grease a 9x13 inch baking dish.
2. In a medium bowl, combine chia seeds, almond butter, applesauce, cinnamon and salt. Mix well.
3. Pour mixture into the prepared baking dish.
4. Bake for 20 minutes or until set. Cool on a wire rack before serving.
5. In a small saucepan over low heat, melt coconut oil or butter. Add sugar and stir until dissolved. Add flour and stir until blended. Cook for 2 minutes longer, stirring constantly. Remove from heat and stir in vanilla extract.
6. Drizzle over pudding when serving.

Storage: It can be stored in BPA Free container for around 4-5 days in the refrigerator and 1-2 months in the freezer. However, if you feel like it smells bad or has an odd texture, then better not to consume it.

Nutrition value per serving: Calories: 528 kcal, Fat: 2 g, Carbs: 10 g, Protein: 2 g, Sugar: 245 mg, Potassium: 200 mg

21 POULTRY RECIPES

21.1 Almond Crusted Chicken Tenders With Honey

Preparation Time: 10 minutes
Cooking Time: 20 minutes
Servings: 4
Ingredients:

- Honey - 1 Tbsp.
- Dijon Mustard – 1 Tbsp.
- Freshly Ground Black Pepper – ¼ Tsp.
- Kosher Or Sea Salt – ¼ Tsp.
- Chicken Breast Tenders Or Tenderloins – 1 Lb.
- Almond Flour – 1 Cup(Chopped)
- Olive Oil – As Needed
- Parsley And Thyme – For Garnish

Procedure:

1. Preheat oven to 400 °F (200 degrees C).
2. Place chicken tenders on baking sheet.
3. In a shallow dish, combine almond flour and salt. Dredge chicken tenders in flour mixture until coated.
4. In a large skillet over medium heat, heat olive oil and honey until warm.
5. Add chicken tenders to skillet; cook for 3 minutes per side or until golden brown and cooked through.
6. Garnish with chopped parsley and thyme; serve hot.

Storage: Can be properly stored in a BPA-free plastic/glass container box for 2 days in the refrigerator and 2-3 months in the freezer.

Nutrition value per serving: Calories: 528 kcal, Fat: 2 g, Carbs: 10 g, Protein: 2 g, Sodium: 245 mg

21.2 Coconut Chicken Tenders

Preparation Time: 10 minutes
Cooking Time: 0 minute
Servings: 4
Ingredients:

- Garlic Powder -1 Tsp
- Boneless Chicken Tenders – 4 Pieces
- Black Pepper – As Needed
- Salt – As needed
- Yogurt – 1 Cup
- Honey – 1 Tbsp.
- Lemon Juice – 1 Tsp.
- Coconut Milk – 1 Cup

Procedure:

1. Preheat oven to 400 °F (200 degrees C).
2. Heat olive oil in a large baking dish.
3. Sprinkle chicken with garlic powder, salt, and black pepper; coat well with yogurt mixture.
4. Bake for 20 minutes or until tender.
5. In a small bowl, whisk together honey, lemon juice, and coconut milk; pour over chicken.
6. Serve warm or cold.

Storage: Can be properly stored in a BPA-free plastic/glass container box for 2 days in the refrigerator and 2-3 months in the freezer.

Nutrition value per serving: Calories: 528 kcal, Fat: 2 g, Carbs: 10 g, Protein: 2 g, Sodium: 245 mg

21.3 Parsley And Dijon Chicken Potatoes

Preparation Time: 10 minutes
Cooking Time: 22 minute
Servings: 4

Ingredients:

- Garlic – 3 Cloves (Minced)
- Freshly Squeezed Lemon Juice – 1 Tbsp. (Freshly Juiced)
- Freshly Ground Black Pepper – ¼ Tsp.
- Yukon Gold Potatoes- 1 And ½ Lb. (Cut Into ½ Inch Cubes)
- Skinless Chicken Thighs – ½ Lb. (Cut Into 1 Inch Cubes)
- Kosher Or Sea Salt – ¼ Tsp.
- Fresh Flat-Leaf (Italian) Parsley, Including Stems
- Extra-Virgin Olive Oil -1 Tbsp.
- Dijon Mustard – 1 Tbsp.
- Cup Dry White Wine – ¼ Cup
- Almond Flour – 1 Cup
- Dill – 1 Tsp.
- Vinegar – 1 Tsp.

Procedure:

1. Preheat oven to 375 degrees.
2. Season the chicken with salt and pepper before dredging it in flour. In a large pan over medium heat, heat the olive oil. Cook until the chicken is golden brown, about 4 minutes per side. Transfer to a baking dish and bake for 25 minutes.
3. Meanwhile, in a large pot of boiling water, add potatoes and 1/2 tsp. salt. Cook until tender, about 15 minutes.
4. Drain potatoes and return them to the pot. Add parsley, dill, vinegar, and remaining salt and pepper; stir well to combine.
5. To serve, divide potatoes among 4 plates. Top with chicken and serve immediately

Storage: Can be properly stored in a BPA-free plastic/glass container box for 2 days in the refrigerator and 2-3 months in the freezer.

Nutrition value per serving: Calories: 528 kcal, Fat: 2 g, Carbs: 10 g, Protein: 2 g, Sodium: 245 mg

21.4 Parmesan Baked Chicken

Preparation Time: 10 minutes
Cooking Time: 20 minutes
Servings: 4

Ingredients:

- Ghee – 2 Tbsp.
- Chicken Breast – 2 Whole (Boneless, Skinless)
- Pink Salt- As Needed
- Fresh Black Pepper- As Needed
- Mayonnaise – ½ Cup
- Parmesan Cheese- 1/2 Cup (Grated)
- Italian Seasoning – 1 Tbsp.
- Pork Rinds – ¼ Cup (Crushed)

Procedure:

1. Pre-heat your oven to 425 degree F
2. Take a large baking dish and coat with ghee
3. Pat chicken breasts dry and wrap with towel
4. Season with salt and pepper
5. Place in baking dish
6. Take a small bowl and add mayonnaise, parmesan cheese, Italian seasoning
7. Slather mayo mix evenly over chicken breast
8. Sprinkle crushed pork rinds on top
9. Bake for 20 minutes until topping is browned
10. Serve and enjoy!

Storage: Can be properly stored in a BPA-free plastic/glass container box for 2 days in the refrigerator and 2-3 months in the freezer.

Nutrition value per serving: Calories: 528 kcal, Fat: 2 g, Carbs: 10 g, Protein: 2 g, Sodium: 245 mg

21.5 Almond Breaded Chicken Delight

Preparation Time: 10 minutes
Cooking Time: 15 minutes
Servings: 4
Ingredients:

- Sunflower Seeds– Just To Taste
- Low-Fat Chicken Broth – 2/3 Cup
- Low Sugar Raspberry Preserve – ½ Cup
- Balsamic Vinegar – 1 And ½ Tbsp.
- Arrowroot - 1 And ½ Tsp.
- Almond Flour – ¼ Cup
- 3 Boneless Chicken Breast– 3 Whole Chicken Breast

Procedure:

1. Discard skin from chicken breasts and season with seeds.
2. To begin, coat each piece of poultry in flour and shake off any excess before frying.
3. Heat a nonstick frying pan to medium-high heat.
4. Serve over rice and steamed broccolini and simmer for 15 minutes, stirring halfway through.
5. Remove the chicken to a serving plate and keep warm.
6. Toss in the arrowroot powder, broth, and raspberry jam to the pan and heat through.
7. For a few minutes, mix in balsamic vinegar and decrease the heat.
8. Return the chicken to the sauce and simmer for a further 15 minutes, stirring occasionally.
9. Serve and savor your meal!

Storage: Can be properly stored in a BPA-free plastic/glass container box for 2 days in the refrigerator and 2-3 months in the freezer.

Nutrition value per serving: Calories: 528 kcal, Fat: 2 g, Carbs: 10 g, Protein: 2 g, Sodium: 245 mg

21.6 Simple Stir Fried Chicken

Preparation Time: 10 minutes
Cooking Time: 12 minutes
Servings: 4
Ingredients:

- Chicken Breast – 2 Large (Boneless and Skinless)
- Lemon Juice – 1/3 Cup
- Almond Meal – 1 and ½ Cups
- Coconut Oil – 2 Tbsp.
- Lemon Pepper – To taste
- Parsley – For garnish

Procedure:

1. Cut the chicken breasts in half and pound each piece until they are about ¼ inch thick.
2. In a pan over medium heat, add coconut oil and allow it to heat up.
3. Dip each piece of chicken breast into lemon juice, letting it sit for 2 minutes on each side.
4. Transfer the lemon-soaked chicken to the almond meal, making sure to coat both sides well.
5. Carefully place the coated chicken in the heated oil and fry for 4 minutes per side, generously sprinkling lemon pepper on each side.
6. Once cooked, transfer the chicken to a paper towel-lined plate to remove excess oil.
7. Repeat the process with the remaining chicken pieces.
8. Garnish with fresh parsley and serve.

Storage: Can be properly stored in a BPA-free plastic/glass container box for 2 days in the refrigerator and 2-3 months in the freezer.

Nutrition value per serving: Calories: 528 kcal, Fat: 34 g, Carbs: 10 g, Protein: 48 g, Sodium: 245 mg

21.7 Blackberry Chicken Wings

Preparation Time: 10 minutes
Cooking Time: 45 minute
Servings: 4

Ingredients:

- Chicken Wings – 3 lb. (20 Pieces)
- Blackberry Chipotle Jam – ½ Cup
- Salt And Pepper – To Taste
- Water – ½ Cup

Procedure:

1. In a bowl, combine the water and blackberry chipotle jam, mixing well.
2. Place the chicken wings in a zip-top bag and add two-thirds of the marinade.
3. Season with salt and pepper, then let the wings marinate for 30 minutes.
4. Preheat your oven to 400°F (204°C).
5. Prepare a baking sheet with a wire rack, and arrange the marinated chicken wings on the rack.
6. Bake the wings for 15 minutes, then brush on the remaining marinade.
7. Continue to bake the wings for an additional 30 minutes, or until fully cooked and slightly caramelized.
8. Serve and enjoy!

Storage: Can be properly stored in a BPA-free plastic/glass container box for 2 days in the refrigerator and 2-3 months in the freezer.

Nutrition value per serving: Calories: 237 kcal, Fat: 15 g, Carbs: 17 g, Protein: 30 g, Sodium: 245 mg

21.8 Amazing Chicken Sheekh Kebab

Preparation Time: 10 minutes
Cooking Time: 10 minute
Servings: 4

Ingredients:

- Wooden Skewers – 6 Pieces
- White Vinegar - ¼ Cup
- Salt – ¼ Tsp.
- Olive Oil – ¼ Cup
- Lemon Juice – ¼ Cup
- Ground Cumin – 1 Tsp. (Ground)
- Ground Black Pepper – ¼ Tsp.
- Green/Red Bell Peppers– 2 Large (Cut Into 1 Inch Pieces)
- Garlic Cloves – 2 Cloves (Minced)
- Fresh Mushrooms - 12 Whole
- Dried Thyme – ½ Tsp.
- Dried Oregano – 1 Tsp. (Ground)
- Cherry Tomatoes – 12 Whole
- Boneless And Skinless Chicken– 2 Lb. (Cut Into 1 And ½ Inch Pieces)

For Sauce

- Tahini Sauce – 1 Cup
- Lemon Juice – 1 Tbsp.
- Garlic Powder – 1 Tsp.

Procedure:

1. Preheat your grill to medium heat.
2. Brush the chicken breast with some olive oil or cooking spray and season it with the spices and herbs listed above
3. Thread the chicken into skewers, alternative between the meat and vegetables
4. Grill the chicken for about 4 minutes per side or until cooked through.
5. Remove from the grill and let cool slightly before slicing into thin strips.
6. In a bowl, mix together tahini sauce, lemon juice and garlic powder until well combined.
7. Serve immediately and enjoy with the sauce mix

Storage: Can be properly stored in a BPA-free plastic/glass container box for 2 days in the refrigerator and 2-3 months in the freezer.

Nutrition value per serving: Calories: 290 kcal, Fat: 13 g, Carbs: 10 g, Protein: 33 g, Sodium: 245 mg

21.9 Awesome Chicken Bell Pepper Platter

Preparation Time: 10 minutes
Cooking Time: 30 minute
Servings: 4

Ingredients:

- Water – ½ Cup
- Tomato – 1 Whole.
- Skinless And Boneless Diced Chicken Breast Halves – 6 Halves (Skinless, Boneless, Diced)
- Salt And Pepper – As Needed
- Red Onion – 1 Whole (Diced)
- Olive Oil – 3 Tbsp.
- Red Bell Pepper– 1 (Whole)
- Dried Oregano, Rosemary, Thyme, Garlic Powder – 2 Tsp. Each

Procedure:

1. Preheat oven to 375 °F. In a small bowl, combine garlic, rosemary, thyme and pepper. Rub mixture all over chicken breasts.
2. Heat a large skillet over medium heat.
3. Add oil and swirl to coat.
4. Add chicken breasts and cook for about 3 minutes per side or until browned.
5. Transfer to a baking dish and bake for about 20 minutes or until cooked through. Meanwhile, in a medium bowl, combine tomatoes, red onion and bell pepper.
6. Drizzle with olive oil and sprinkle with salt and parsley leaves. Serve the chicken atop the vegetables.

Storage: Can be properly stored in a BPA-free plastic/glass container box for 2 days in the refrigerator and 2-3 months in the freezer.

Nutrition value per serving: Calories: 336 kcal, Fat: 10 g, Carbs: 26 g, Protein: 35 g, Sodium: 245 mg

21.10 Cheesy Chicken Nuggets

Preparation Time: 10 minutes
Cooking Time: 5 minutes
Servings: 4

Ingredients:

- Chicken Breast – 1 Whole (Pre-Cooked)
- Parmesan Cheese – ½ Oz. (Grated_
- Almond Flour – 2 Tbsp.
- Baking Powder – ½ Tsp.
- Egg – 1 Whole
- Water – 1 Tbsp.

Procedure:

1. Cut breast into bite sized portions
2. Take a bowl and add parmesan, flour, baking powder, water
3. Mix well
4. Cover chicken pieces in batter
5. Take a skillet and place it over medium heat, add oil and let it heat up
6. Add chicken nuggets and fry until golden brown
7. Serve and enjoy!

Storage: Can be properly stored in a BPA-free plastic/glass container box for 2 days in the refrigerator and 2-3 months in the freezer.

Nutrition value per serving: Calories: 230 kcal, Fat: 6 g, Carbs: 2 g, Protein: 28 g, Sodium: 245 mg

21.11 Simple And Wholesome Baked Chicken Breast

Preparation Time: 10 minutes
Cooking Time: 40 minute
Servings: 4

Ingredients:

- Skinless And Boneless Chicken Breast – 2 Whole (8 Ounces Each, Skinless And Boneless)
- Salt– As Needed
- Olive Oil – ¼ Cup
- Ground Black Pepper – As Needed
- Freshly Squeezed Lemon Juice – ¼ Cup
- Dried Thyme - ¼ Tsp.
- Dried Oregano - ½ Tsp.
- Chicken Broth – 1 Cup
- Vinegar – 1 Tsp.
- Honey – 1 Tsp.
- Parsley – 1 Tsp.

Procedure:

1. In a small bowl, whisk together the oil, oregano, thyme, salt and pepper. Rub the mixture all over the chicken breast.
2. Place in a baking dish. Pour the chicken broth over the chicken and bake for 25 minutes, or until cooked through. Let cool for 5 minutes before serving.
3. Stir in the vinegar and honey and garnish with parsley leaves.

Storage: Can be properly stored in a BPA-free plastic/glass container box for 2 days in the refrigerator and 2-3 months in the freezer.

Nutrition value per serving: Calories: 501 kcal, Fat: 32 g, Carbs: 3 g, Protein: 47 g, Sodium: 245 mg

21.12 Chicken And Basil Zucchini Noodles

Preparation Time: 10 minutes
Cooking Time: 10 minutes
Servings: 4

Ingredients:

- Zucchini – 1 Whole (Shredded)
- Garlic- 1 Clove (Peeled And Minced)
- Coconut Milk – ¼ Cup
- Basil – ½ Cup (Chopped)
- Tomatoes – 1 Lb. (Diced)
- Ghee – 2 Tbsp.
- Chicken Fillets – 2 Whole (Cubed)

Procedure:

1. Saute cubed chicken in ghee until no longer pink
2. Add tomatoes and season with salt
3. Simmer and reduce liquid
4. Prepare your zucchini Noodles by shredding zucchini in food processor
5. Add basil, garlic, coconut milk to chicken and cook for a few minutes
6. Add half of the zucchini Zoodles to a bowl and top with creamy tomato basil chicken
7. Enjoy!

Storage: Can be properly stored in a BPA-free plastic/glass container box for 2 days in the refrigerator and 2-3 months in the freezer.

Nutrition value per serving: Calories: 724 kcal, Fat: 26 g, Carbs: 81 g, Protein: 3 g, Sodium: 245 mg

21.13 Bacon And Chicken Garlic Wrap

Preparation Time: 10 minutes
Cooking Time: 10 minutes
Servings: 4
Ingredients:

- Chicken Fillet - 1 Whole (Cut Into Small Cubes)
- Bacon Slices – 8-9 Slices (Cut Into Cubes)
- Garlic – 6 Cloves (Minced)

Procedure:

1. Pre-heat your oven to 400 degree F
2. Line a baking tray with aluminum foil
3. Add minced garlic to a bowl and rub each chicken piece with it
4. Wrap bacon piece around each garlic chicken bite
5. Secure with toothpick
6. Transfer bites to baking sheet, keeping a little bit of space between them
7. Bake for about 15-20 minutes until crispy
8. Serve and enjoy!

Storage: Can be properly stored in a BPA-free plastic/glass container box for 2 days in the refrigerator and 2-3 months in the freezer.

Nutrition value per serving: Calories: 724 kcal, Fat: 26 g, Carbs: 81 g, Protein: 3 g, Sodium: 245 mg

21.14 Hearty Chicken Breast Salad

Preparation Time: 10 minutes
Cooking Time: 30-40 minutes
Servings: 4
Ingredients:

- Spinach – 2 Tbsp.
- Olive Oil – 2 Tbsp.
- Lettuces – 1 And ¾ Oz.
- Lemon Juice To Taste – To Taste
- Chicken Breast – 3 And ½ Oz.
- Bell Pepper – 1 Whole

Procedure:

1. Boil chicken breast without adding salt cut the meat into small strips
2. Put the spinach in boiling water for a few minutes, cut into small strips
3. Cut pepper in strips as well
4. Add everything to a bowl and mix with juice and oil
5. Serve!

Storage: Can be properly stored in a BPA-free plastic/glass container box for 2 days in the refrigerator and 2-3 months in the freezer.

Nutrition value per serving: Calories: 724 kcal, Fat: 26 g, Carbs: 81 g, Protein: 3 g, Sodium: 245 mg

22 RED MEAT DISHES RECIPES

22.1 Cool Medi Grilled Lamb Chops

Preparation Time: 10 minutes
Cooking Time: 10 minutes
Servings: 4

Ingredients:

- Olive Oil – ½ Cup
- Lamb Shoulder Chops – 4 Whole (8 Ounces Each)
- Ground Black Pepper – ¼ Tsp.
- Garlic – 1 Tbsp.
- Fresh Basil – 2 Tbsp.
- Dijon Mustard – 2 Tbsp.
- Balsamic Vinegar – 2 Tbsp.

Procedure:

1. Pat the lamb chops dry first and arrange them on a shallow glass baking dish
2. Take a bowl and whisk in Dijon mustard, garlic, balsamic vinegar and pepper
3. Mix them well
4. Whisk oil slowly into the marinade until it is smooth
5. Stir in basil
6. Pour the whole marinade over the lamb chops, making sure to coat both sides
7. Cover and allow the chops to marinate for 1-4 hours
8. Bring the chops to room temperature and leave them for 30 minutes
9. Pre-heat your grill to medium heat and oil up your grate
10. Grill the lamb chops until they are nicely browned (giving 5-10 minutes) per side
11. Grill until the center read 145 degree Fahrenheit
12. Enjoy!

Storage: Can be properly stored in a BPA-free plastic/glass container box for 2 days in the refrigerator and 2-3 months in the freezer.

Nutrition value per serving: Calories: 528 kcal, Fat: 2 g, Carbs: 10 g, Protein: 2 g, Sugar: 245 mg, Potassium: 255 mg

22.2 Foil Ala Pork

Preparation Time: 10 minutes
Cooking Time: 25 minutes
Servings: 4

Ingredients:

- Salt And Pepper To Taste – As Needed
- Raw Ham – 4 Slices
- Pork Chops– 4 Whole (2 Oz. Each)
- Onion – 1 Oz.
- Olive Oil To Taste – As Needed
- Garlic – 1 Clove
- Cooking Cream – 4 Tbsp.
- Champignon Mushrooms – 10 Oz.

Procedure:

1. Wash and dry the pork ribs.
2. Remove the earthy part of the mushrooms and then wash them and dry them then chop them finely.
3. Peel and wash the garlic clove and onion and then chop them.
4. Put a little olive oil in a non-stick pan, and brown for 2 minutes on each side, season with salt and pepper and then set aside.
5. In the same pan, sauté the garlic and onion, stir and as soon as they are golden, add the mushrooms.
6. Cut the ham into strips and then add it to the mushrooms.
7. Season with salt and pepper and cook for 10 minutes.
8. Arrange the pork ribs in 4 aluminum sheets. Brush them with the cooking cream and cover with the mixture of mushrooms and ham.
9. Close the packets and place them in the oven to cook at 356 ° F for 25 minutes.
10. As soon as the pork is cooked, take them out of the oven, let the meat rest for 5 minutes and then remove them from the foil.
11. Put the meat on individual serving plates and serve sprinkled with the mushroom mix and the cooking juices as an accompanying sauce

Storage: Can be properly stored in a BPA-free plastic/glass container box for 2 days in the refrigerator and 2-3 months in the freezer.

Nutrition value per serving: Calories: 528 kcal, Fat: 2 g, Carbs: 10 g, Protein: 2 g, Sugar: 245 mg, Potassium: 255 mg

22.3 Pomegranate Sauce And Pork Fillet

Preparation Time: 10 minutes
Cooking Time: 65 minutes
Servings: 4
Ingredients:

- Salt And Pepper– As Needed
- Rosemary– As Needed
- Pork Tenderloin – 21 Oz.
- Pomegranate Juice Extract – 1 Cup
- Laurel– As Needed
- Garlic- - 1 Clove
- Cornstarch – 2 Tbsp.
- Brown Sugar – 2 Tbsp.
- Bay Leaf – 1-2 whole

Procedure:

1. Wash and dry the fillet with kitchen paper.
2. Wash all the aromatic herbs and peel the garlic clove.
3. Macerate the fillet in pomegranate juice with garlic, rosemary, bay leaf, and pepper.
4. Cover with plastic wrap and place in the fridge for about 2 hours, turning it from time to time.
5. In a pan, heat two tablespoons of olive oil and brown the fillet.
6. Wet it often with the cooking juices.
7. Now, prepare the sauce by filtering the marinating juice, add the sugar and corn starch. Put the sauce on the fire and let it thicken.
8. Place the fillet in a pan brushed with olive oil.
9. Put the baking pan in the oven and cook at 356 9F for about 20 minutes.
10. After 25 minutes, turn the meat and continue cooking for another 20 minutes.
11. As soon as it is cooked, remove the fillet from the oven and let it rest for 5 minutes.
12. Then cut the fillet into slices and place it on serving plates.
13. Drizzle with the pomegranate sauce and serve.

Storage: Can be properly stored in a BPA-free plastic/glass container box for 2 days in the refrigerator and 2-3 months in the freezer.

Nutrition value per serving: Calories: 528 kcal, Fat: 2 g, Carbs: 10 g, Protein: 2 g, Sugar: 245 mg, Potassium: 255 mg

22.4 Juicy Pork Fillet With Aromatic Crust

Preparation Time: 10 minutes
Cooking Time: 10 minute
Servings: 4
Ingredients:

- Speck – 3 And ½ Oz. (Thinly Sliced)
- Salt And Pepper To Taste – As Needed
- Rosemary – 2 Sprigs
- Pork Tenderloin – 21 Oz.
- Parsley – 10 Leaves
- Olive Oil To Taste – As Needed
- Mustard – 2 Tbsp.
- Marjoram - 2 Whole
- Extra Virgin Olive Oil – 2 tbsp.

Procedure:

1. Wash and dry the parsley, rosemary and marjoram and then chop and put them in a bowl.
2. Chop the speck and put it in the bowl with the aromatic herbs.
3. Add the mustard and mix until you get a homogeneous mixture.
4. Wash and dry the pork fillet and then brush the entire surface of the meat with the emulsion.
5. Heat two tablespoons of olive oil in a pan and, when hot, brown the fillet.
6. Brown for 2 minutes on each side, then put the lid on the pan and continue cooking for another 20 minutes.
7. Season with salt and pepper, turn off and let the meat rest for 10 minutes.

8. Now cut the fillet into slices.
9. Put the fillet slices on serving plates, sprinkle them with the cooking juices and serve.

Storage: Can be properly stored in a BPA-free plastic/glass container box for 2 days in the refrigerator and 2-3 months in the freezer.

Nutrition value per serving: Calories: 528 kcal, Fat: 2 g, Carbs: 10 g, Protein: 2 g, Sugar: 245 mg, Potassium: 255 mg

22.5 Grape Sauce And Pork Fillet

Preparation Time: 10 minutes
Cooking Time: 65 minutes
Servings: 4
Ingredients:

- White Grapes – 5 And ½ Oz.
- Thyme – 3 Sprigs
- Thinly Sliced Speck – 2 Oz.
- Salt And Pepper To Taste – As Needed
- Pork Tenderloin – 2 Whole (8 Oz. Each)
- Olive Oil To Taste – As Needed
- Garlic – 2 Cloves
- Black Grapes – 5 And ½ Oz.
- Red Wine – 1 cup

Procedure:

1. Wash and dry the pork tenderloin and remove all excess fat. Season the meat with salt and pepper.
2. Peel and wash the garlic cloves and then chop them.
3. Wash and let the grapes drain.
4. Heat 3 tablespoons of olive oil in a pan and, when hot, brown the garlic cloves.
5. Add the fillet and brown it for two minutes on each side.
6. Brush a baking pan with olive oil and, when the fillet is golden on the outside, put it in the baking pan with all the cooking juices.
7. Wash and dry the thyme and put it in the baking pan with the meat.
8. Wet the meat with the wine, put the baking pan in the oven and cook at 320 0 F for 35 minutes.
9. After cooking, remove the baking pan from the oven.
10. Remove the meat from the baking pan and wrap it in aluminum foil.
11. Put the pork juices in a pan.
12. Add the minced speck and brown it until crisp.
13. Now add the grapes and sauté for 4 minutes.
14. Now cut the fillet into slices and place it on serving plates.
15. Sprinkle with the grape sauce and serve.

Storage: Can be properly stored in a BPA-free plastic/glass container box for 2 days in the refrigerator and 2-3 months in the freezer.

Nutrition value per serving: Calories: 528 kcal, Fat: 2 g, Carbs: 10 g, Protein: 2 g, Sugar: 245 mg, Potassium: 255 mg

22.6 Pork With Gorgonzola Sauce

Preparation Time: 10 minutes
Cooking Time: 65 minutes
Servings: 4
Ingredients:

- Vegetable Cream – 1 Glass
- Sprig Rosemary – 1 Sprig
- Speck – 8 Slices
- Salt And Pepper To Taste – As Needed
- Pork Tenderloin In One Piece – 2 Whole (8 Oz. Each)
- Olive Oil To Taste – As Needed
- Gorgonzola – 2 Whole (8 Oz Each)

Procedure:

1. Wash and dry the pork fillet and then massage the entire surface of the meat with salt and pepper.
2. Cut the fillet into 4 slices of the same size.
3. Wrap the meat with the slices of speck and then tie the meat with kitchen string.
4. Wash the sprig of rosemary and divide it into four parts.
5. Put the rosemary between the kitchen string and the meat.
6. Brush the surface of the meat with olive oil and then put it in a baking pan brushed with olive oil.

7. Cook the fillets at 356 ° for 20 minutes, then turn the fillets and continue cooking for another 35 minutes.
8. Once cooked, remove the baking pan from the oven and let the meat rest for 10 minutes.
9. Then move on to prepare the accompanying sauce.
10. Cut the gorgonzola into cubes and put it in a saucepan with the cream.
11. Put the saucepan on the stove and cook until the cheese has completely melted, and the sauce has taken on a thick and homogeneous consistency.
12. At this point, remove the kitchen string and cut the meat into slices.
13. Put the meat on serving plates, sprinkle them with the gorgonzola sauce and serve.

Storage: Can be properly stored in a BPA-free plastic/glass container box for 2 days in the refrigerator and 2-3 months in the freezer.

Nutrition value per serving: Calories: 528 kcal, Fat: 2 g, Carbs: 10 g, Protein: 2 g, Sugar: 245 mg, Potassium: 255 mg

22.7 Fennel And Figs Lamb

Preparation Time: 10 minutes

Cooking Time: 40 minutes

Servings: 4

Ingredients:

- Swerve – 1 Tbsp.
- Apple Cider Vinegar – 1/8 Cup
- Figs – 4 (Cut In Half)
- Olive Oil – 2 Tbsp.
- Salt And Pepper – As Needed
- Fennel Bulbs – 2 Whole, Sliced
- Lamb Rack – 12 Oz.

Procedure:

1. Take a bowl and add fennel, figs, vinegar, swerve, oil and toss
2. Transfer to baking dish
3. Season with salt and pepper
4. Bake for 15 minutes at 400 degree F
5. Season lamb with salt and pepper and transfer to a heated pan over medium-high heat
6. Cook for a few minutes
7. Add lamb to baking dish with fennel and bake for 20 minutes
8. Divide between plates and serve
9. Enjoy!

Storage: Can be properly stored in a BPA-free plastic/glass container box for 2 days in the refrigerator and 2-3 months in the freezer.

Nutrition value per serving: Calories: 528 kcal, Fat: 2 g, Carbs: 10 g, Protein: 2 g, Sugar: 245 mg, Potassium: 255 mg

22.8 Spicy Paprika Lamb Chops

Preparation Time: 10 minutes
Cooking Time: 15 minutes
Servings: 4

Ingredients:

- Chili Powder – 1 Tsp.
- Cumin Powder – ¾ Cup
- Paprika – 3 Tbsp.
- Salt And Pepper- As Needed
- Lamb Racks – 2 Whole (Cut Into Chops)

Procedure:

1. Take a bowl and add paprika, cumin, chili, salt, pepper and stir
2. Add lamb chops and rub the mixture
3. Heat grill over medium-temperature and add lamb chops, cook for 5 minutes
4. Flip and cook for 5 minutes more, flip again
5. Cook for 2 minutes, flip and cook for 2 minutes more
6. Serve and enjoy!

Storage: Can be properly stored in a BPA-free plastic/glass container box for 2 days in the refrigerator and 2-3 months in the freezer.

Nutrition value per serving: Calories: 528 kcal, Fat: 2 g, Carbs: 10 g, Protein: 2 g, Sugar: 245 mg, Potassium: 255 mg

22.9 Coconut And Almond Beef

Preparation Time: 10 minutes
Cooking Time: 50 minutes
Servings: 4

Ingredients:

- Parsley – For Garnish
- Cumin – 1 Tsp.
- Chili Powder – 1Tsp.
- Sugar Free Coconut Milk – 2 Cups
- Shallot – 1 Whole
- Salt And Pepper To Taste – As Needed
- Olive Oil To Taste – As Needed
- Beef Fillet – 2 Whole (8 Oz. Each, Ground)
- Almonds – ¼ cup (Sliced)

Procedure:

1. Preheat oven to 350 °F (175 degrees C).
2. In a large bowl, combine ground beef, coconut milk, olive oil, cumin, chili powder, and salt. Mix well until all ingredients are well combined.
3. Transfer mixture to a baking dish and bake for 30-35 minutes, or until beef is cooked through.
4. Garnish with parsley and almonds before serving. Enjoy!

Storage: Can be properly stored in a BPA-free plastic/glass container box for 2 days in the refrigerator and 2-3 months in the freezer.

Nutrition value per serving: Calories: 528 kcal, Fat: 2 g, Carbs: 10 g, Protein: 2 g, Sugar: 245 mg, Potassium: 255 mg

22.10 Beef And Red Onion Stew

Preparation Time: 10 minutes + 2 Hours Of Marinating
Cooking Time: 2 hours
Servings: 4

Ingredients:

- White Wine – 1 Glass
- Salt And Pepper To Taste – As Needed
- Red Onions – 2 Whole
- Olive Oil To Taste – As Needed
- Carrot – 1 Whole
- Beef Rump – 2 Whole (8 Oz. Each)
- Basil Leaves – 4 Leaves, Chopped

Procedure:

1. First you can peel and wash the carrot and then chop it.
2. Wash and dry the rump of beef, then tie it with kitchen twine.
3. Massage the meat with salt and pepper and then put it in a bowl.
4. Add the carrot, chopped basil and white wine
5. Put the bowl in the refrigerator and let it marinate for 2 hours.
6. After this time, remove the bowl from the fridge and bring it back to room temperature.

Storage: Can be properly stored in a BPA-free plastic/glass container box for 2 days in the refrigerator and 2-3 months in the freezer.

Nutrition value per serving: Calories: 528 kcal, Fat: 2 g, Carbs: 10 g, Protein: 2 g, Sugar: 245 mg, Potassium: 255 mg

22.11 Beef Sirloin With Juniper

Preparation Time: 10 minutes
Cooking Time: 10 minutes
Servings: 4

Ingredients:

- Salt And Pepper To Taste – As Needed
- Olive Oil To Taste – As Needed
- Juniper Berries – 2 Oz.
- Garlic – 3 Cloves
- Beef Sirloin – 2 Whole (8 Oz. Each)
- Balsamic Vinegar – 2 Tbsp.

Procedure:

1. sprinkle it with salt and pepper.
2. Peel and wash the garlic cloves and then chop them.
3. Heat two tablespoons of olive oil and when it is hot, put the garlic to fry.
4. Add the juniper berries, balsamic vinegar, salt, and pepper, stir, and then turn off.
5. Place the sirloin in a bowl and cover it with the marinade.
6. Cover the bowl and leave to marinate for an hour.
7. After the hour, heat a grill and when it is hot, put the meat to grill.
8. Cook for 4 minutes on each side, then remove it from the grill and put it to rest on a cutting board.
9. Cut the sirloin into slices and place them on serving plates.
10. Sprinkle with the marinating liquid and serve.

Storage: Can be properly stored in a BPA-free plastic/glass container box for 2 days in the refrigerator and 2-3 months in the freezer.

Nutrition value per serving: Calories: 528 kcal, Fat: 2 g, Carbs: 10 g, Protein: 2 g, Sugar: 245 mg, Potassium: 255 mg

23 SAUCES, DIPS AND DRESSING RECIPES

23.1 Classic Basil Pesto

Preparation Time: 10 minutes
Cooking Time: 10 minute
Servings: 1 cup

Ingredients:

- Salt – A Pinch
- Pine Nuts - ¼ Cups (Raw And Unsalted)
- Parmesan Cheese – ¾ Cups (Shredded)
- Garlic - 2 Cloves (Peeled And Halved)
- Extra-Virgin Olive Oil – 5 Tbsp.
- Black Pepper – A Pinch
- Basil Leaves– 1 And 1/2 Cups

Procedure:

1. In a food processor, combine all of the ingredients except parmesan cheese and parsley
2. Process until ingredients are finely chopped.
3. Mix in Parmesan cheese and parsley.
4. Serve with pasta or use as a condiment for grilled meats or fish.

Storage: Ideally, the sauce can be stored in a container for up to 5-6 days. And it can be stored properly in the freezer for up to 6 months, as long as it does not contain any ingredients such as cheese or eggs.

Nutrition value per serving: Calories: 528 kcal, Fat: 2 g, Carbs: 10 g, Protein: 2 g, Sugar: 245 mg, Potassium: 200 mg

23.2 Pesto Rosso

Preparation Time: 10 minutes
Cooking Time: 5 minutes
Servings: 1 and ½ cups

Ingredients:

- Salt - Pinch
- Black Pepper – Pinch
- Extra Virgin Olive Oil – ¾ Cup
- Garlic– 3 Cloves (Peeled And Halved)
- Sun Dried Tomatoes- 1 Cup
- Almond – 1/3 Cup (Roasted And Unsalted)
- Fresh Rosemary – 1 Tbsp.
- Basil Leaves – 1 Cup (Chopped)

Procedure:

1. In a food processor, pulse the listed ingredients thoroughly until you have a fine mix
2. Pour pesto into a small serving bowl and enjoy.

Storage: Ideally, the sauce can be stored in a container for up to 5-6 days. And it can be stored properly in the freezer for up to 6 months, as long as it does not contain any ingredients such as cheese or eggs.

Nutrition value per serving: Calories: 528 kcal, Fat: 2 g, Carbs: 10 g, Protein: 2 g, Sugar: 245 mg, Potassium: 200 mg

23.3 Leafy Green Pesto

Preparation Time: 10 minutes
Cooking Time: 5 minutes
Servings: 1 cup

Ingredients:

- Salt – Pinch
- Parmesan– ½ Cup (Shredded)
- Kale – 1 Cup
- Garlic– 3 Cloves (Peeled And Halved)
- Extra-Virgin Olive Oil – ½ Cup
- Black Pepper - Pinch
- Baby Spinach Leaves – 1 Cup
- Almonds– ¼ Cup (Raw And Unsalted)

Procedure:

1. Place all the ingredients into a food processor, pulse until smooth, then serve.

Storage: Ideally, the sauce can be stored in a container for up to 5-6 days. And it can be stored properly in the freezer for up to 6 months, as long as it does not contain any ingredients such as cheese or eggs.

Nutrition value per serving: Calories: 528 kcal, Fat: 2 g, Carbs: 10 g, Protein: 2 g, Sugar: 245 mg, Potassium: 200 mg

23.4 Authentic Tomato Sauce

Preparation Time: 10 minutes
Cooking Time: 60 minutes
Servings: 1 cup
Ingredients:

- Sugar – 1 Tsp.
- Salt – Pinch
- Plum Tomatoes, – 4 Lb. (Quartered)
- Green/Red Bell Pepper – 1 Whole (Diced)
- Garlic– 4 Cloves (Peeled And Diced)
- Extra-Virgin Olive Oil - Tbsp.
- Black Pepper – Pinch
- Onion – 1 Whole (Diced)
- Fresh Oregano – 1 Tbsp.
- Fresh Lime Juice – 1 Tsp.

Procedure:

1. In a large pot or Dutch oven, heat the oil over medium heat. Add the onion and bell pepper and cook until softened, about 5 minutes.
2. Add the garlic and sugar and cook for 1 minute longer.
3. Stir in the tomatoes with their juice, oregano, black pepper, and lime juice. Bring to a simmer and cook until thickened, about 10 minutes. Serve hot.

Storage: Ideally, the sauce can be stored in a container for up to 5-6 days. And it can be stored properly in the freezer for up to 6 months, as long as it does not contain any ingredients such as cheese or eggs.

Nutrition value per serving: Calories: 528 kcal, Fat: 2 g, Carbs: 10 g, Protein: 2 g, Sugar: 245 mg, Potassium: 200 mg

23.5 Avocado Cream

Preparation Time: 10 minutes
Cooking Time: 10 minute
Servings: 1 cup
Ingredients:

- Salt – Pinch
- Garlic – 3 Cloves (Minced)
- Fresh Lime Juice – 3 Tbsp. (Fresh)
- Black Pepper – Pinch
- 2 Avocados– 2 Whole (Halved And Pitted)
- Full-Fat Greek Yogurt – 1 Cup

Procedure:

1. Add all the ingredients into a food processor. Pulse until evenly combined and smooth, then serve.

Storage: Ideally, the sauce can be stored in a container for up to 5-6 days. And it can be stored properly in the freezer for up to 6 months, as long as it does not contain any ingredients such as cheese or eggs.

Nutrition value per serving: Calories: 528 kcal, Fat: 2 g, Carbs: 10 g, Protein: 2 g, Sugar: 245 mg, Potassium: 200 mg

23.6 Original Tzatziki

Preparation Time: 10 minutes
Cooking Time: 15 minutes
Servings: 1 cup
Ingredients:

- Salt - Pinch
- White Pepper - Pinch
- Black Pepper - Pinch
- White Wine Vinegar - 1 Tsp.
- Garlic – 4 Cloves (Minced)
- English Cucumber – 1 Medium
- Full-Fat Greek Yogurt – 2 Cups

Procedure:

1. Grate the cucumber and place it into a strainer. Over the kitchen sink, press the cucumber down with a spoon, so any extra liquid can drain. Then, transfer onto a kitchen towel.
2. Combine the remaining ingredients and then add the cucumber. Seal in an

airtight container and allow to chill in the refrigerator for two hours.
3. Remove from the refrigerator and then serve.

Storage: Ideally, the sauce can be stored in a container for up to 5-6 days. And it can be stored properly in the freezer for up to 6 months, as long as it does not contain any ingredients such as cheese or eggs.

Nutrition value per serving: Calories: 528 kcal, Fat: 2 g, Carbs: 10 g, Protein: 2 g, Sugar: 245 mg, Potassium: 200 mg

23.7 The Salsa Verde Classic

Preparation Time: 10 minutes
Cooking Time: 5 minutes
Servings: 1 cup
Ingredients:

- Salt – Pinch
- Black Pepper – Pinch
- Extra-Virgin Olive Oil – 8 Tbsp.
- Lemon Juice – 1 And ½ Tbsp.
- Dijon Mustard – 1 Tsp.
- Garlic – 1 Clove
- Capers, Drained And Rinsed – 3 Tbsp.
- Mint Leaves– 1 And ½ Oz. (Diced)
- Flat-Leaf Parsley– 1 And ½ Oz. (Diced)

Procedure:

1. Place the garlic, capers, mint, and parsley onto a chopping board. Using a sharp knife, dice together until a rough paste is formed.
2. Scoop the paste into a bowl and add the salt, pepper, olive oil, lemon juice, and mustard. Combine, then serve.

Storage: Ideally, the sauce can be stored in a container for up to 5-6 days. And it can be stored properly in the freezer for up to 6 months, as long as it does not contain any ingredients such as cheese or eggs.

Nutrition value per serving: Calories: 528 kcal, Fat: 2 g, Carbs: 10 g, Protein: 2 g, Sugar: 245 mg, Potassium: 200 mg

23.8 Harissa

Preparation Time: 10 minutes
Cooking Time: 5 minutes
Servings: ½ cup
Ingredients:

- Tomato Puree – 1 Tsp.
- Salt – Pinch
- Saffron Threads - Pinch
- Red Pepper – 1 Whole (Roasted)
- Red Chilis-2 Whole (Deseeded And Diced)
- Ground Coriander - Pinch
- Cayenne Pepper - Pinch
- Black Pepper – Pinch

Procedure:

1. Add all the ingredients into a food processor, pulse until smooth, then serve.

Storage: Ideally, the sauce can be stored in a container for up to 5-6 days. And it can be stored properly in the freezer for up to 6 months, as long as it does not contain any ingredients such as cheese or eggs.

Nutrition value per serving: Calories: 528 kcal, Fat: 2 g, Carbs: 10 g, Protein: 2 g, Sugar: 245 mg, Potassium: 200 mg

23.9 Trapanese

Preparation Time: 10 minutes
Cooking Time: 5 minutes
Servings: 1 cup

Ingredients:

- Salt - Pinch
- Parmesan Cheese – ½ Cup (Shredded)
- Garlic, Diced – 1 Clove (Diced)
- Extra-Virgin Olive Oil – ½ Cup
- Cherry Tomatoes – 1 Cup
- Black Pepper – Pinch
- Basil Leaves – 2 And ½ Cups
- Almonds– ¼ Cup (Raw And Unsalted)

Procedure:

1. In a small frying pan over medium heat, add the almonds. Toast them for one minute, then remove from heat.
2. Add the almonds and garlic into a food processor and pulse until smooth.
3. Add the tomatoes and basil to the mixture and pulse. As the machine is pulsing, slowly add in the olive oil until smooth.
4. Follow by adding in the salt, pepper, and Parmesan. Pulse until smooth.
5. Remove from the food processor and serve.

Storage: Ideally, the sauce can be stored in a container for up to 5-6 days. And it can be stored properly in the freezer for up to 6 months, as long as it does not contain any ingredients such as cheese or eggs.

Nutrition value per serving: Calories: 528 kcal, Fat: 2 g, Carbs: 10 g, Protein: 2 g, Sugar: 245 mg, Potassium: 200 mg

23.10 Almond Butter Chocolate Dip

Preparation Time: 10 minutes
Cooking Time: 0 minute
Servings: 4

Ingredients:

- Vanilla - 1 Tsp.
- Plain Greek Yogurt – 1 Cup
- Honey – 1 Tbsp.
- Chocolate Hazelnut Spread – 1/3 Cup
- Almond Butter – ½ Cup

Procedure:

1. Take a medium sized microwave proof bowl, add the listed ingredients and gently stir
2. Microwave the mixture for around 1-2 minutes until everything has melted
3. Mix again and enjoy!

Storage: Ideally, the sauce can be stored in a container for up to 5-6 days. And it can be stored properly in the freezer for up to 6 months, as long as it does not contain any ingredients such as cheese or eggs.

Nutrition value per serving: Calories: 115 kcal, Fat: 8 g, Carbs: 15 g, Protein: 4 g, Sodium: 245 mg

24 DESSERTS

24.1 Black Tea Cake

Preparation Time: 10 minutes
Cooking Time: 35 minutes
Servings: 4

Ingredients:

- Vanilla Extract – 2 Tsp.
- Stevia - 2 Cups
- Eggs – 4 Whole
- Black Tea Powder – 6 Tbsp.
- Baking Soda – 1 Tsp.
- Baking Powder - 3 Tsp.
- Avocado Oil – 1 Cup
- Almond Milk– 2 Cups
- Almond Flour – 3 And ½ Cups

Procedure:

1. Set the oven to preheat at 350°F. Apply grease and flour to an 8x8-inch baking pan. Combine the flour, baking powder, and salt in a separate bowl by sifting them together.
2. In a large mixing bowl, use an electric mixer at medium speed to cream the butter and sugar until the mixture becomes smooth and fluffy.
3. Incorporate the eggs into the mixture one at a time, making sure to mix well after adding each egg.
4. Blend in the black tea powder and raisins. Slowly introduce the dry ingredients to the wet ingredients, mixing only until combined. Pour the batter into the prepared baking pan.
5. Bake the cake for 30 minutes or until a toothpick inserted in the center comes out clean. Allow the cake to cool in the pan for 10 minutes before transferring it to a wire rack to cool completely.

Storage: It can be stored in BPA Free container for around 4-5 days in the refrigerator and 1-2 months in the freezer. However, if you feel like it smells bad or has an odd texture, it is better not to consume it.

Nutrition value per serving: Calories: 505 kcal, Fat: 38 g, Carbs: 20 g, Protein: 15 g, Sugar: 1 g, Sodium: 410 mg, Potassium: 85 mg

24.2 Tasty Figs Pie

Preparation Time: 10 minutes
Cooking Time: 60 minutes
Servings: 4

Ingredients:

- Figs – 6 whole (cut in quarters) -
- Vanilla extract – ½ tsp.
- Almond flour – 1 cup
- Eggs – 4 (whisked)
- Sugar – 1 cup
- Cinnamon – 1 tsp.

Procedure:

1. Preheat oven to 375 °F (190 degrees C).
2. In a medium bowl, combine figs, sugar, flour, cinnamon, nutmeg and salt. Toss until coated.
3. Pour mixture into the pie crust.
4. Dot with butter and oil. Bake for 15 minutes or until the filling is bubbly. Let cool before serving.

Storage: It can be stored in BPA Free container for around 4-5 days in the refrigerator and 1-2 months in the freezer. However, if you feel like it smells bad or has an odd texture, it is better not to consume it.

Nutrition value per serving: Calories: 528 kcal, Fat: 2 g, Carbs: 10 g, Protein: 2 g, Sugar: 245 mg, Potassium: 222 mg

24.3 Dark Chocolate Mousse

Preparation Time: 10 minutes
Cooking Time: 10 minute
Servings: 4

Ingredients:

- Unsweetened Dark Chocolate– 3 And ½ Oz (Grated)
- Vanilla – ½ Tsp.
- Honey – 1 Tbsp.
- Greek Yogurt – 2 Cups
- Unsweetened Almond Milk – ¾ Cup
- Fresh Raspberries – For Garnish

Procedure:

1. Add chocolate and almond milk in a saucepan and heat over medium heat until just chocolate melted. Do not boil.
2. Once the chocolate and almond milk combined then add vanilla and honey and stir well.
3. Add yogurt in a large mixing bowl.
4. Pour chocolate mixture on top of yogurt and mix until well combined.
5. Pour chocolate yogurt mixture into the serving bowls and place in refrigerator for 2 hours.
6. Top with fresh raspberries and serve.

Storage: It can be stored in a BPA Free container for around 4-5 days in the refrigerator and 1-2 months in a freezer. However, if you feel like it smells bad or has an odd texture, then better not to consume it.

Nutrition value per serving: Calories: 528 kcal, Fat: 2 g, Carbs: 10 g, Protein: 2 g, Sugar: 245 mg, Potassium: 200 mg

24.4 Apple And Plum Cake

Preparation Time: 10 minutes
Cooking Time: 40 minutes
Servings: 4

Ingredients:

- Zest Of Lemon– 1 Whole (Grated)
- Warm Almond Milk – 3 Oz.
- Stevia – 5 Tbsp.
- Plums– 2 Lb. (Pitted And Cut Into Sections)
- Egg– 1 Whole (Whisked)
- Walnuts – ½ cup (slived)
- Baking Powder – 1 Tsp.
- Apples - 2 Whole (Cored And Chopped)
- Almond Flour – 7 Oz.
- Sugar – 1 cup
- Flour – 1 cup
- Olive oil – as needed

Procedure:

1. Preheat oven to 350 °F (175 degrees C).
2. Grease and flour one 9x13 inch baking pan.
3. In a medium bowl, whisk together the sugar, flour, baking powder, and salt; set aside.
4. In a large bowl, combine the oil, eggs and apples; mix well. Add the flour mixture to the apple mixture, mixing well until well combined.
5. Stir in the plums and nuts.
6. Pour batter into prepared pan. Bake for 30 minutes or until a toothpick inserted into center comes out clean.
7. Cool cake in pan for 10 minutes before removing to a wire rack to cool completely.

Storage: It can be stored in BPA Free container for around 4-5 days in the refrigerator and 1-2 months in the freezer. However, if you feel like it smells bad or has an odd texture, it is better not to consume it.

Nutrition value per serving: Calories: 528 kcal, Fat: 2 g, Carbs: 10 g, Protein: 2 g, Sugar: 245 mg, Potassium: 222 mg

24.5 Cinnamon And Chickpea Cookies

Preparation Time: 10 minutes
Cooking Time: 0 minute
Servings: 4
Ingredients:

- Stevia – ½ Cup
- Raisins – 1 Cup
- Egg– 1 Whole (Whisked)
- Coconut– 1 Cup
- Cinnamon Powder – 1 Tsp.
- Chickpeas– 1 Cup (Drained, Rinsed And Mashed)
- Baking Powder – 1 Tsp.
- Avocado Oil – 1 Cup
- Almond Flour – 2 Cups
- Almond Extract – 2 Tsp.
- Vanilla Extract – 1 Tsp.

Procedure:

1. Preheat oven to 350 °F (175 degrees C). Line a baking sheet with parchment paper.
2. In a food processor, blend chickpeas until they are smooth. In a medium bowl, whisk all ingredients except vanilla extract
3. Pour chickpea mixture into the bowl and blend until just combined. With the food processor still running, add oil or butter and egg.
4. Blend until dough forms. Add vanilla extract and mix until well combined. Drop dough by rounded tablespoons onto prepared baking sheet. Bake for 12 minutes, or until cookies are golden brown around the edges.
5. Allow cookies to cool on baking sheet for 5 minutes before transferring to a wire rack to cool completely. Enjoy!

Storage: It can be stored in BPA Free container for around 12-14 days in the refrigerator and 1-2 months in the freezer

Nutrition value per serving: Calories: 528 kcal, Fat: 2 g, Carbs: 10 g, Protein: 2 g, Sugar: 245 mg, Potassium: 222 mg

24.6 Hearty Lemon Mousse

Preparation Time: 10 minutes
Cooking Time: 10 minutes +Chill Time
Servings: 4
Ingredients:

- 1 cup coconut cream
- 8 ounces cream cheese, soft
- ¼ cup fresh lemon juice
- 3 pinches salt
- 1 teaspoon lemon liquid stevia

Procedure:

1. Pre-heat your oven to 350-degree F
2. Grease a ramekin with butter
3. Beat cream, cream cheese, fresh lemon juice, salt and lemon liquid stevia in a mixer
4. Pour batter into ramekin
5. Bake for 10 minutes then transfer mouse to serving glass
6. Let it chill for 2 hours and serve
7. Enjoy!

Storage: It can be stored in BPA Free container for around 4-5 days in the refrigerator and 1-2 months in the freezer. However, if you feel like it smells bad or has an odd texture, it is better not to consume it.

Nutrition value per serving: Calories: 528 kcal, Fat: 2 g, Carbs: 10 g, Protein: 2 g, Sugar: 245 mg, Potassium: 222 mg

24.7 Spicy Poached Pears

Preparation Time: 10 minutes
Cooking Time: 17 minute
Servings: 4

Ingredients:

- Whole Star Anise - 1 Whole
- Whole Garlic Cloves – 2 Cloves
- Water – 3 And ½ Cups
- Vanilla Extract – 1 Tsp.
- Semi Ripe Pears (Preferably Barlett Pears) – 3 Whole (Semi Ripe)
- Rind Of Lemon – 1
- Juice Of Lemon – 1
- Granulated Sugar – 3 Cups
- Cinnamon Sticks – 2 Sticks

Procedure:

1. Peel the pears well and keep them on the side
2. Take a pot of water and add vanilla, lemon juice, sugar, lemon rind, cinnamon sticks, cloves and star anise
3. Place it over medium heat and allow the sugar to dissolve
4. Add pears
5. Lower down the heat to low and simmer for another 15-20 minutes
6. Once the pears are ready, transfer to a Tupperware alongside the cooking liquid
7. Allow it to cool
8. Enjoy!

Storage: It can be stored in BPA Free container for around 12-14 days in the refrigerator and 1-2 months in the freezer.

Nutrition value per serving: Calories: 740 kcal, Fat: 4 g, Carbs: 18 g, Protein: 4 g, Sugar: 245 mg, Potassium: 222 mg

24.8 Pineapple And Ginger Sherbet

Preparation Time: 10 minutes
Cooking Time: 0 minute
Servings: 4

Ingredients:

- Pineapple Chunks – 8 Oz.
- Ground Ginger – ¼ Tsp.
- Vanilla – ¼ Tsp.
- Orange Sections – 11 Oz.
- Pineapple, Lemon Or Lime Sherbet – 2 Cups
- Cornstarch – 1 tsp.
- Ginger – 1 tsp. (grated)
- Sugar – ½ cup
- Cinnamon – 1 tsp. (ground)
- Salt and pepper – as needed

Procedure:

1. Combine pineapple, ginger, sugar, cornstarch, cinnamon and salt in a blender; blend until smooth.
2. Pour mixture into a saucepan over medium heat; bring to a boil.
3. Cook for 2 minutes or until thickened.
4. Add cold water and lemon sherbet; stir well. Serve immediately.

Storage: Can be stored in juice/drinks container for 2-3 days.

Nutrition value per serving: Calories: 267 kcal, Fat: 1 g, Carbs: 65 g, Protein: 2 g, Sugar: 245 mg, Potassium: 222 mg

24.9 Awesome Peach And Raspberry Trifle

Preparation Time: 10-20 minutes
Cooking Time: 0 minutes
Servings: 4
Ingredients:

- Trifle Sponge Cake– 1 Whole (Cut Into Pieces)
- Punnet Fresh Raspberries – 5 Oz.
- Peaches - 28 Oz.
- Mascarpone – 2 And ½ Cups
- Limoncello Liqueur, Sherry Or Brandy – ½ Cup
- Hazlenuts - 14 Cup (Chopped)
- Custard – 2 Cups

Procedure:

1. Take a bowl and add custard and mascarpone
2. Place about half of your sponge cake piece into the large serving bowl
3. Drizzle ¼ cup of sherry, Limoncello or brandy
4. Cover with drained up peach slices
5. Add half of the custard mix
6. Keep repeating the process (making the layers) until the mixture has been used up
7. Keep in mind that you are to end with the mascarpone layer
8. Chill and serve!
9. Top with some peaches, raspberries of hazelnut if you wish
10. Enjoy!

Storage: It can be stored in BPA Free container for around 4-5 days in the refrigerator and 1-2 months in the freezer. However, if you feel like it smells bad or has an odd texture, it is better not to consume it.

Nutrition value per serving: Calories: 472 kcal, Fat: 34 g, Carbs: 40 g, Protein: 8 g, Sugar: 245 mg, Potassium: 222 mg

24.10 Five Berry Compote

Preparation Time: 10 minutes
Cooking Time: 10 minute
Servings: 4
Ingredients:

- Water – ½ Cup
- Vanilla - 1 Tsp.
- Sugar – 2/3 Cup
- Strawberries– 1 Cup
- Sprig Fresh Mints – 3 Sprigs
- Sauvignon Blanc – 1 Bottle
- Red Raspberries – 1 Cup
- Pomegranate Juice – ½ Cup
- Orange Pekoe Tea Bags – 3 Bags
- Golden Raspberries – 1 Cup
- Fresh Sweet Cherries – 1 Cup (Pitted And Halved)
- Fresh Mint Sprigs
- Fresh Blueberries – 1 Cup
- Fresh Black Berries – 1 Cup

Procedure:

1. Take a small saucepan and add water
2. Bring the water to a boil and add tea bags, 3 mint sprigs
3. Stir well
4. Cover pan and remove the heat
5. Allow it to stand for 10 minutes
6. Take a large sized bowl and add strawberries, red raspberries, golden raspberries, blueberries, blackberries, cherries. Keep it on the side
7. Take a medium sized saucepan and add wine, sugar, pomegranate juice
8. Pour the infusion (tea mixture) through a fine mesh sieve and into the pan with wine
9. Squeeze the bags to release the liquid
10. Discard the mint sprigs and tea bags
11. Cook well until the sugar has completely dissolved
12. Remove the heat
13. Stir in vanilla and allow it to chill for 2 hours
14. Pour the mix over the fruits
15. Serve by garnishing with some mint sprigs
16. Enjoy!

Storage: It can be stored in BPA Free container for around 4-5 days in the refrigerator and 1-2 months in the freezer. However, if you feel like it smells bad or has an odd texture, it is better not to consume it.

Nutrition value per serving: Calories: 203 kcal, Fat: 0 g, Carbs: 34 g, Protein: 1 g, Sugar: 245 mg, Potassium: 222 mg

24.11 Dreamy Hot Fudge

Preparation Time: 10 minutes
Cooking Time: 5- 10 minutes
Servings: 4
Ingredients:

- ½ cup salted butter
- 4 ounces dark chocolate
- 2 tablespoons unsweetened cocoa powder
- 1 cup swerve
- 1 cup heavy whip cream
- 2 teaspoons vanilla extract
- Pinch of salt

Procedure:

1. Take a medium saucepan and place it over medium heat
2. Add butter and chocolate and melt
3. Add cocoa powder and sweetener
4. Whisk for 3-5 minutes until everything dissolves
5. Add cream and bring to a boil
6. Stir
7. Lower down heat to low and add vanilla and salt
8. Remove heat
9. Let it sit for 5 minutes
10. Serve hot and enjoy!

Storage: It can be stored in BPA Free container for around 4-5 days in the refrigerator and 1-2 months in the freezer. However, if you feel like it smells bad or has an odd texture, it is better not to consume it.

Nutrition value per serving: Calories: 256 kcal, Fat: 20 g, Carbs: 17 g, Protein: 6 g, Sugar: 245 mg, Potassium: 222 mg

24.12 Perfect Frozen Strawberry Yogurt

Preparation Time: 10 minutes
Cooking Time: 2-4 Hours
Servings: 4
Ingredients:

- Vanilla – 2 Tsp.
- Sugar – 1 Cup
- Strawberries - 1 Cup (Sliced)
- Salt – 1/8 Tsp.
- Greek Low-Fat Yogurt – 3 Cups
- Freshly Squeeze Lemon Juice – ¼ Cup

Procedure:

1. Take a medium sized bowl and add yogurt, lemon juice, sugar, vanilla and salt
2. Whisk the whole mixture well
3. Freeze the yogurt mix in a 2 quart ice cream maker according to the given instructions
4. Make sure to add sliced strawberries during the final minute
5. Transfer the yogurt to an air tight container
6. Freeze for another 2-4 hours
7. Allow it to stand for about 5-15 minutes
8. Serve and enjoy!

Storage: It can be stored in BPA Free container for around 4-5 days in the refrigerator and 1-2 months in the freezer. However, if you feel like it smells bad or has an odd texture, it is better not to consume it.

Nutrition value per serving: Calories: 86 kcal, Fat: 1 g, Carbs: 16 g, Protein: 86 g, Sugar: 245 mg, Potassium: 222 mg

24.13 Simple Chocolate Parfait

Preparation Time: 10 minutes +2 Hours
Cooking Time: 0 minute
Servings: 4
Ingredients:

- Cocoa Powder – 2 Tbsp.
- Almond Milk – 1 Cup
- Chia Seeds – 1 Tbsp.
- Vanilla Extract – ½ Tsp.

Procedure:

1. In a bowl, combine cocoa powder, almond milk, chia seeds, and vanilla extract. Mix well.
2. Transfer the mixture to dessert glasses and refrigerate for 2 hours
3. Serve and enjoy!

Storage: It can be stored in BPA Free container for around 4-5 days in the refrigerator and 1-2 months in the freezer. However, if you feel like it smells bad or has an odd texture, it is better not to consume it.

Nutrition value per serving: Calories: 72 kcal, Fat: 4 g, Carbs: 7 g, Protein: 3 g, Sugar: 2 g, Potassium: 89 mg

24.14 Perfect Blueberry Muffins

Preparation Time: 10 minutes
Cooking Time: 20-25 minutes
Servings: 4
Ingredients:

- Almond Flour – 1 Cup
- Salt – A Pinch
- Baking Soda – 1/8 Tsp.
- Egg- 1 Whole
- Coconut Oil – 2 Tbsp, Melted
- Coconut Milk – ½ Cup
- Fresh Blueberries – ¼ Cup

Procedure:

1. Preheat your oven to 350°F (180°C).
2. Line a muffin tin with paper muffin cups.
3. In a bowl, combine almond flour, salt, and baking soda; set aside.
4. In another bowl, mix together the egg, coconut oil, and coconut milk.
5. Add the wet ingredients to the dry ingredients and gently combine until incorporated.
6. Fold in the blueberries and fill the muffin cups with batter.
7. Bake for 20-25 minutes or until a toothpick inserted in the center comes out clean.
8. Enjoy!

Storage: It can be stored in BPA Free container for around 4-5 days. Storage in the freezer is not recommended.

Nutrition value per serving: Calories: 230 kcal, Fat: 19 g, Carbs: 10 g, Protein: 6 g, Sugar: 3 g, Potassium: 50 mg

25 SNACKS RECIPES

25.1 Hearty Almond Cracker

Preparation Time: 15 minutes
Cooking Time: 15-20 minute
Servings: 4

Ingredients:

- Almond Flour – 1 Cup
- Baking Soda – ¼ tsp.
- Salt – ¼ tsp.
- Black Pepper – 1/8 Tsp.
- Sesame Seeds – 3 Tbsp.
- Egg – 1 Whole (Beaten)
- Salt And Pepper – Taste

Procedure:

1. Heat the oven to 350°F (180°C) and prepare two baking sheets by lining them with parchment paper.
2. Combine all dry ingredients in a large mixing bowl, then incorporate the beaten egg to create a dough.
3. Separate the dough into two equal parts.
4. Using two sheets of parchment paper, roll each dough portion to the desired thickness.
5. Cut the dough into the desired cracker shapes and arrange them on the lined baking sheets.
6. Place the crackers in the oven and bake for 15-20 minutes or until they become golden brown and crisp.
7. Continue this process until all of the dough has been used.
8. Allow the baked crackers to cool down before serving.
9. Enjoy your homemade almond crackers!

Nutrition value per serving: Calories: 210 kcal, Fat: 17 g, Carbs: 6 g, Protein: 8 g, Sodium: 260 mg

25.2 Baby Braised Artichokes

Preparation Time: 10 minutes
Cooking Time: 30 minutes
Servings: 6

Ingredients:

- Olive Oil - 6 Tbsp.
- Baby Artichokes – 2 Lb.
- Lemon Juice – ½ Cup
- Garlic Cloves – 4 Cloves (Sliced)
- Salt And Pepper – ½ Tsp.
- Tomatoes – 1 And ½ Lb. (Seeded And Diced)
- Almonds - ½ Cup (Sliced)
- Oregano – 1 tbsp.

Procedure:

1. Preheat oven to 400 degrees.
2. Cut off the top of each artichoke and cut in half lengthwise.
3. Drop artichokes into boiling water for one minute to shock them.
4. Drain artichokes and place in a large baking dish.
5. Pour chicken broth over artichokes and sprinkle with black pepper, olive oil, lemon juice, oregano, thyme, salt and pepper.
6. Bake for 30 minutes or until artichokes are tender when pierced with a fork.
7. Garnish with sliced almonds
8. Enjoy!

Storage: It can be stored in BPA Free container for around 4-5 days in the refrigerator and 1-2 months in the freezer.

Nutrition value per serving: Calories: 220 kcal, Fat: 18 g, Carbs: 15 g, Protein: 4 g, Sodium: 245 mg

25.3 Kale And Mozzarella Egg Bake

Preparation Time: 10 minutes
Cooking Time: 36 minutes
Servings: 4

Ingredients:

- Salt And Pepper – To Taste
- Spike Seasoning – 1 Tsp.
- Eggs – 8 Whole
- Green Onion – 1/3 Cup, Sliced
- Mozzarella Cheese – 1 And ½ Cup (Grated)

Procedure:

1. Pre-heat your oven to 375 degree F
2. Prepare a casserole dish by greasing lightly with olive oil
3. Take a skillet and place it over medium heat, let it get hot
4. Add kale and cook for 3 minutes
5. Add kale to prepared casserole dish
6. Spread it well
7. Top kale with onions, cheese
8. Crack eggs into medium bowl and season with salt and pepper, spike seasoning
9. Whisk well and pour into casserole dish
10. Stir
11. Bake in your oven for 35 minutes until eggs set and become golden brown
12. Serve and enjoy!

Storage: It can be stored in BPA Free container for around 4-5 days in the refrigerator and 1-2 months in the freezer.

Nutrition value per serving: Calories: 124 kcal, Fat: 8 g, Carbs: 4 g, Protein: 10 g, Sodium: 200 mg

25.4 Crunchy And Delicious Fougasse

Preparation Time: 10 minutes
Cooking Time: 30 minutes
Servings: 4

Ingredients:

- Bread Flour – 3 And 2/3 Cups
- Olive Oil – 3 And ½ Tbsp.
- Bread Yeast – 1 And 2/3 Tbsp.
- Black Olives– 1 And ½ Cups (Chopped)
- Oregano – 1 Tsp.
- Salt – ½ Tbsp.
- Water - 1 Cup

Procedure:

1. Take a bowl and add flour
2. Form a volcano in the center by making a well and add the remaining ingredients (alongside water)
3. Knead the dough well until it becomes slightly elastic
4. Mold it into a ball and let it stand for about 1 hour
5. Divide the pastry into four pieces of equal portions
6. Flatten the balls using a rolling pin
7. Place the balls on a floured baking tray
8. Make incisions on the bread as shown in the picture
9. Allow them to rest for about 30 minutes
10. Pre-heat your oven to a temperature of 428 Fahrenheit
11. Brush the Fougasse with olive oil and allow it to bake for 20 minutes
12. Turn the oven off and allow it to rest for 5 minutes
13. Remove and allow it to cool
14. Enjoy!

Storage: It can be stored in BPA Free container for around 4-5 days in the refrigerator and 1-2 months in the freezer. However, if you feel like it smells bad or has an odd texture, it is better not to consume it.

Nutrition value per serving: Calories: 560 kcal, Fat: 18 g, Carbs: 30 g, Protein: 57 g, Sodium: 245 mg

25.5 Italy's Fan Favorite Herb Bread

Preparation Time: 10 minutes
Cooking Time: 40 minutes
Servings: 25
Ingredients:

- Active Dry Yeast – 2 And ½ Tsp.
- All-Purpose Flour – 3 And ½ Cups
- Rye Flour – 2 And ¼ Cups
- Salt – 1 Tsp.
- Olive Oil – 2 Tbsp.
- Flat Leaf Parsley – 1 Tbsp.
- Fresh Thyme– 10 Sprigs
- Garlic - 1 Whole (Peeled And Chopped)
- Black Olives – ¼ Cup (Pitted And Chopped)
- Jalapenos - 3 Whole (Chopped And Deseeded)
- Sun Dried Tomatoes– ¾ Cup (Drained And Chopped)

Procedure:

1. Take a bowl of lukewarm water (temperature of 105°F) and dissolve 1 and a 2/3 cups of yeast
2. Add flour, yeast, water and salt to another bowl
3. Mix well to prepare the dough using a mixer or with your hands
4. Take a large-sized clean bowl and add the dough to the bowl. Allow it to rest covered for 2 hours
5. Transfer it to your lightly floured surface and knead the dough (alongside parsley, garlic, olives, thyme, tomatoes, and chilies) and knead well to mix everything
6. Place the kneaded dough onto an 8 and a ½ inch bread proofing basket
7. Cover it and allow it to rest for about 60 minutes
8. Pre-heat your oven to a temperature of 400 °F
9. Line up a baking sheet with parchment paper
10. Bake for about 30-40 minutes
11. Enjoy once done!

Storage: It can be stored in BPA Free container for around 4-5 days in the refrigerator and 1-2 months in the freezer.

Nutrition value per serving: Calories: 90 kcal, Fat: 2 g, Carbs: 16 g, Protein: 2 g, Sodium: 245 mg

25.6 Cheesy And Creamy Broccoli And Cauliflower

Preparation Time: 10 minutes
Cooking Time: 10 minutes
Servings: 4
Ingredients:

- Sour Cream – 4 Tsp.
- Salt And Pepper – As Needed
- Parmesan Cheese- 5 Oz. (Shredded)
- Cauliflower – 8 Oz. (Chopped)
- Butter – 2 Oz.
- Broccoli – 1 Lb. (Chopped)

Procedure:

1. Take a large skillet and melt butter
2. Stir in all the vegetables
3. Sauté until it turns into golden brown over medium-high heat
4. Add all the remaining ingredients to the vegetable
5. Mix well and cook until the cheese melts
6. Serve warm, and enjoy!

Storage: It can be stored in BPA Free container for around 4-5 days in the refrigerator and 1-2 months in the freezer.

Nutrition value per serving: Calories: 244 kcal, Fat: 10 g, Carbs: 5 g, Protein: 6 g, Sodium: 200 mg

25.7 Classic Focaccia

Preparation Time: 40 minutes
Cooking Time: 40 minute
Servings: 4

Ingredients:

- Flour – 3 And ½ Cups
- Warm Water – 1 And ¼ Cups
- Olive Oil – 2 Tbsp.
- Baker's Yeast – 2 Tsp. + Salt And Sugar To Activate The Yeast
- Tsp. Of Salt - 1 And ½ Tsp.
- Black Olives – 14 Oz. (Chopped)
- Sea Salt– As Needed
- Olive Oil– As Needed
- Butter – 1 Cup

Procedure:

1. Preheat the oven to 375 °F (190 degrees C). Grease a baking sheet and dust with flour.
2. Take a glass and add warm water, add yeast and let it sit for 10 minutes to activate it with a bit of salt and sugar
3. In a large bowl, mix together the flour and salt, olive oil, black olive. Cut in the butter until the mixture resembles coarse crumbs. Stir in the water until a soft dough forms.
4. Turn out the dough onto a lightly floured surface and knead for about 5 minutes. Place the dough in a greased bowl, turning it to coat with oil. Cover with plastic wrap and let rise in a warm place for 30 minutes.
5. Punch down the dough and divide into 12 equal parts. Shape each part into a 6-inch round loaf, tucking the ends under as you go. Place on the prepared baking sheet and let rise for another 20 minutes.
6. Bake for 25 minutes, until golden brown. Let cool on a wire rack before slicing into thick slices.

Storage: It can be stored in BPA Free container for around 4-5 days in the refrigerator and 1-2 months in the freezer.

Nutrition value per serving: Calories: 510 kcal, Fat: 13 g, Carbs: 86 g, Protein: 11 g, Sodium: 245 mg

25.8 Tasty Zucchini Chips

Preparation Time: 10 minutes
Cooking Time: 15 minute
Servings: 4

Ingredients:

- Olive oil – 1 tbsp.
- Salt – 1 tsp.
- Black pepper – ¼ tsp.
- Parmesan cheese – ¼ cup
- Romano cheese – ¼ cup
- Zucchini – 1 whole (cut into thin chips)
- Panko bread crumbs – ½ cup

Procedure:

1. Preheat the oven to 400 °F.
2. In a large bowl, mix together the salt, black pepper, Parmesan cheese, and Romano cheese.
3. Add the zucchini chips and olive oil and mix until combined. Spread mixture onto a baking sheet and bake for 18 minutes, or until golden brown.
4. Remove from oven and let cool for 5 minutes before topping with panko bread crumbs. Enjoy!

Nutrition value per serving: Calories: 528 kcal, Fat: 2 g, Carbs: 10 g, Protein: 2 g, Sodium: 245 mg

26 MEAL PLAN

I prepared a meal plan for 10 weeks which is about 2 1/2 months. Repeating this meal plan 5-6 times throughout the year, starting from the first week after the tenth, you will have concluded your annual nutrition plan. To ensure the habit of this diet and the results, we recommend applying it for 3 years, consequently for a total of 1000 days.

26.1 Week 1

Days	Breakfast	Lunch	Dinner	Dessert
1	Bacon And Brie Omelet Wedges	Kidney Beans And Cilantro Salad	Homely Fattoush Salad	Black Tea Cake
2	Vegetarian Shepherd's Pie	Mediterranean Pepper Soup	Lovely Onion Soup	Hearty Lemon Mousse
3	Fresh Watermelon And Arugula Meal	Mashed Beans And Cumin	Black Bean With Mangoes	Pineapple And Ginger Sherbet
4	Dill And Tomato Frittata	Bulgar Pila With Garbanzo Bean	Turkish Canned Pinto Bean Salad	Spicy Poached Pears
5	Classic Focaccia	Pecan Crusted Trout	Spicy Cajun Shrimp	Cinnamon And Chickpea Cookies
6	Tasty Zucchini Chips	Lebanese Thin Pasta	Mushroom And Fettucine Platter	Dark Chocolate Mousse
7	Eggs And Acorn In A Hole	Creamy Millet Dish	Tuna And Olive Pasta	Apple And Plum Cake

26.2 Week 2

Days	Breakfast	Lunch	Dinner	Dessert
1	Fresh Watermelon And Arugula Meal		Salsa Rice Meal	Tasty Figs Pie
2	Morning Scrambled Pesto Salad	Stuffed Avocado Meal	Fried Cauliflower Pizza	Frozen Strawberry Yogurt
3	Italy's Favorite Herb Bread	Parmesan Baked Chicken	Tomato Bruschetta	Perfect Blueberry Muffin
4	Tasty Zucchini Chips	Simple Stir Fried Chicken	Yogurt And Banana Bowl	Simple Chocolate Parfait
5		Foil Ala Pork	Chia And Almond Butter Pudding	Apple And Plum Cake
6	Black Olive Breakfast Loaf	Coconut And Almond Beef	Awesome Chicken Bell Pepper Platter	Tasty Figs Pie
7	Vegetarian Shepherd's Pie	Spicy Poached Pears	Bacon And Chicken Garlic Wrap	Awesome Peach And Raspberry Trifle

26.3 Week 3

Days	Breakfast	Lunch	Dinner	Dessert
1	Crunchy And Delicious Fougasse	Beef Sirloin With Juniper		Cinnamon And Chickpea Cookies
2	Dill And Tomato Frittata	Spicy Paprika Lamb	Coconut Almond Beef	Spicy Poached Pears
3	Egg And Acorn In A Hole	Blackberry Chicken Wings	Simple Stir Fried Chicken	Dreamy Hot Fudge
4	Tasty Zucchini Chips		Tuna And Olive Pasta	Perfect Frozen Strawberry Yogurt
5	Fancy Olive And Cheese Loaf	Creamy Rice Millet Dish	Red Chicken Spaghetti	Perfect Blueberry Muffins
6	Morning Scrambled Pesto Eggs	Pesto And Lemon Halibut	Pecan Crusted Trout	Five Berry Compote
7	Fresh Watermelon And Arugula Meal	Orange And Herbed Sauce White Bass	One-Pot Seafood Chowder	Pineapple And Ginger Sherbet

26.4 Week 4

Days	Breakfast	Lunch	Dinner	Dessert
1	Fresh Watermelon And Arugula Meal	Avocado And Chimichurri Bruschetta	Salsa Rice Meal	Tasty Figs Pie
2	Morning Scrambled Pesto Salad	Stuffed Avocado Meal		Frozen Strawberry Yogurt
3	Italy's Favorite Herb Bread	Parmesan Baked Chicken	Tomato Bruschetta	Perfect Blueberry Muffin
4	Tasty Zucchini Chips		Yogurt And Banana Bowl	Simple Chocolate Parfait
5	Dill And Tomato Frittata	Foil Ala Pork	Chia And Almond Butter Pudding	Apple And Plum Cake
6	Black Olive Breakfast Loaf	Coconut And Almond Beef	Awesome Chicken Bell Pepper Platter	Tasty Figs Pie
7	Vegetarian Shepherd's Pie	Spicy Poached Pears	Bacon And Chicken Garlic Wrap	Awesome Peach And Raspberry Trifle

26.5 Week 5

Days	Breakfast	Lunch	Dinner	Dessert
1	Bacon And Brie Omelet Wedges	Kidney Beans And Cilantro Salad	Homely Fattoush Salad	Black Tea Cake
2	Vegetarian Shepherd's Pie	Mediterranean Pepper Soup		Hearty Lemon Mousse
3	Fresh Watermelon And Arugula Meal		Black Bean With Mangoes	Pineapple And Ginger Sherbet
4	Dill And Tomato Frittata	Bulgar Pila With Garbanzo Bean	Turkish Canned Pinto Bean Salad	Spicy Poached Pears
5	Classic Focaccia	Pecan Crusted Trout	Spicy Cajun Shrimp	Cinnamon And Chickpea Cookies
6	Tasty Zucchini Chips	Lebanese Thin Pasta	Mushroom And Fettucine Platter	Dark Chocolate Mousse
7	Eggs And Acorn In A Hole	Creamy Millet Dish	Tuna And Olive Pasta	Apple And Plum Cake

26.6 Week 6

Days	Breakfast	Lunch	Dinner	Dessert
1	Crunchy And Delicious Fougasse	Beef Sirloin With Juniper	Grape Sauce And Pork Fillet	Cinnamon And Chickpea Cookies
2	Dill And Tomato Frittata		Coconut Almond Beef	Spicy Poached Pears
3	Egg And Acorn In A Hole	Blackberry Chicken Wings	Simple Stir Fried Chicken	Dreamy Hot Fudge
4	Tasty Zucchini Chips	Chicken Bruschetta Burgers	Tuna And Olive Pasta	
5	Fancy Olive And Cheese Loaf	Creamy Rice Millet Dish	Red Chicken Spaghetti	Perfect Blueberry Muffins
6	Morning Scrambled Pesto Eggs	Pesto And Lemon Halibut	Pecan Crusted Trout	Five Berry Compote
7	Fresh Watermelon And Arugula Meal	Orange And Herbed Sauce White Bass	One-Pot Seafood Chowder	Pineapple And Ginger Sherbet

26.7 Week 7

Days	Breakfast	Lunch	Dinner	Dessert
1	Fresh Watermelon And Arugula Meal	Avocado And Chimichurri Bruschetta	Salsa Rice Meal	Tasty Figs Pie
2	Morning Scrambled Pesto Salad		Fried Cauliflower Pizza	Frozen Strawberry Yogurt
3	Italy's Favorite Herb Bread	Parmesan Baked Chicken	Tomato Bruschetta	Perfect Blueberry Muffin
4	Tasty Zucchini Chips	Simple Stir Fried Chicken	Yogurt And Banana Bowl	Simple Chocolate Parfait
5	Dill And Tomato Frittata	Foil Ala Pork	Chia And Almond Butter Pudding	
6	Black Olive Breakfast Loaf		Awesome Chicken Bell Pepper Platter	Tasty Figs Pie
7	Vegetarian Shepherd's Pie	Spicy Poached Pears	Bacon And Chicken Garlic Wrap	Awesome Peach And Raspberry Trifle

26.8 Week 8

Days	Breakfast	Lunch	Dinner	Dessert
1	Crunchy And Delicious Fougasse	Beef Sirloin With Juniper	Grape Sauce And Pork Fillet	Cinnamon And Chickpea Cookies
2	Dill And Tomato Frittata		Coconut Almond Beef	Spicy Poached Pears
3	Egg And Acorn In A Hole	Blackberry Chicken Wings	Simple Stir Fried Chicken	Dreamy Hot Fudge
4	Tasty Zucchini Chips	Chicken Bruschetta Burgers	Tuna And Olive Pasta	Perfect Frozen Strawberry Yogurt
5	Fancy Olive And Cheese Loaf	Creamy Rice Millet Dish	Red Chicken Spaghetti	Perfect Blueberry Muffins
6	Morning Scrambled Pesto Eggs	Pesto And Lemon Halibut	Pecan Crusted Trout	Five Berry Compote
7	Fresh Watermelon And Arugula Meal	Orange And Herbed Sauce White Bass		Pineapple And Ginger Sherbet

26.9 Week 9

Days	Breakfast	Lunch	Dinner	Dessert
1	Fresh Watermelon And Arugula Meal	Avocado And Chimichurri Bruschetta	Salsa Rice Meal	Tasty Figs Pie
2	Morning Scrambled Pesto Salad	Stuffed Avocado Meal	Fried Cauliflower Pizza	Frozen Strawberry Yogurt
3	Italy's Favorite Herb Bread	Parmesan Baked Chicken	Tomato Bruschetta	Perfect Blueberry Muffin
4	Tasty Zucchini Chips	Simple Stir Fried Chicken	Yogurt And Banana Bowl	Simple Chocolate Parfait
5	Dill And Tomato Frittata	Foil Ala Pork	Chia And Almond Butter Pudding	Apple And Plum Cake
6	Black Olive Breakfast Loaf	Coconut And Almond Beef	Awesome Chicken Bell Pepper Platter	Tasty Figs Pie
7	Vegetarian Shepherd's Pie	Spicy Poached Pears	Bacon And Chicken Garlic Wrap	Awesome Peach And Raspberry Trifle

26.10 Week 10

Days	Breakfast	Lunch	Dinner	Dessert
1	Bacon And Brie Omelet Wedges	Kidney Beans And Cilantro Salad	Homely Fattoush Salad	Black Tea Cake
2	Vegetarian Shepherd's Pie	Mediterranean Pepper Soup	Lovely Onion Soup	Hearty Lemon Mousse
3	Fresh Watermelon And Arugula Meal	Mashed Beans And Cumin	Black Bean With Mangoes	Pineapple And Ginger Sherbet
4	Dill And Tomato Frittata	Bulgar Pila With Garbanzo Bean	Turkish Canned Pinto Bean Salad	Spicy Poached Pears
5	Classic Focaccia	Pecan Crusted Trout	Spicy Cajun Shrimp	Cinnamon And Chickpea Cookies
6	Tasty Zucchini Chips	Lebanese Thin Pasta	Mushroom And Fettucine Platter	Dark Chocolate Mousse
7	Eggs And Acorn In A Hole	Creamy Millet Dish	Tuna And Olive Pasta	Apple And Plum Cake

27 MEASUREMENT CONVERSION CHART

Weight volumes

US STANDARD	EU STANDARD
½ oz.	15 g
1 oz.	30 g
2 oz.	60g
3 oz.	90 g
4oz.	125g
6 oz.	175g
8 oz.	250g
10 oz.	300g
12 oz.	375 g
13 oz.	400 g
14 oz.	425 g
1 lb	500 g
1½ lb	750 g
2 lb	1 kg

Dry Volumes

US STANDARD	EU STANDARD
1/8 teaspoon	0.5 mL
1/4 teaspoon	1 mL
1/2 teaspoon	2 mL
3/4 teaspoon	4 mL
1 teaspoon	5 mL
1 tablespoon	15 mL
1/4 cup	59 mL
1/2 cup	118 mL
3/4 cup	177 mL
1 cup	235 mL
2 cups	475 mL
3 cups	700 mL
4 cups	1 L

Liquid volume

US STANDARD	US STANDARD (OUNCES)	METRIC (APPROX.)
2 tablespoons	1 fl. oz.	30 mL
1/4 cup	2 fl. oz.	60 mL
1/2 cup	4 fl. oz.	120 mL
1 cup	8 fl. oz.	240 mL
1 1/2 cup	12 fl. oz.	355 mL
2 cups or 1 pint	16 fl. oz.	475 mL
4 cups or 1 quart	32 fl. oz.	1 L
1 gallon	128 fl. oz.	4 L

Temperature

US STANDARD	EU STANDARD
225 °F	107 °C
250 °F	120 °C
275 °F	135 °C
300 °F	150 °C
325 °F	160 °C
350 °F	180 °C
375 °F	190 °C
400 °F	205 °C
425 °F	220 °C
450 °F	235 °C
475 °F	245 °C
500 °F	260 °C

CONCLUSION

I would like to thank you for taking the time and reading this book through to the end. I sincerely hope that you found the information within this book to be interesting and valuable. The Mediterranean Diet is a diet that combines foods from the regions of the Mediterranean, including Greece, Turkey, and Lebanon. This diet is one of the best for overall health and weight loss. The diet is low in saturated fat, high in monounsaturated fats, and low in sodium. The diet includes lots of fruits, vegetables, whole grains, olive oil, and fish. This diet has risen in popularity, and for a good reason. This diet is known for its health benefits, including lower heart disease and cancer rates, improved mental health, and reduced stress levels. It is also low in calories, which can help you lose weight or maintain a healthy weight. The diet also benefits pregnant women and young children by providing enough essential nutrients and calories to stay healthy. The diet's focus on fruits and vegetables, whole grains, legumes, cheese, and seafood, is linked with a lower risk of heart disease. The diet has been linked with a lower risk of stroke, hypertension, arthritis, diabetes, and death from any cause. In addition, the diet is good for your blood sugar control and can help improve your cholesterol levels. And those are just the tip of the iceberg because, as you know now, the diet not only focuses on healthy eating but also helps you to develop a healthy lifestyle by encouraging you to engage in more social activities with friends and families while partaking in a physical workout every day. In short, the Mediterranean diet is the complete package for anyone who wants to lead a hassle-free healthy life while not having to sacrifice the awesome and delicious foods of life. Keeping that in mind, I wish you all the best for the journey ahead!

BONUS: Scanning the following QR code will take you to a web page where you can access 5 fantastic
bonuses after leaving your email contact: Body Fat Calculator, Body Mass Index Calculator, Daily Caloric Needs Calculator, 2 mobile apps for iOS and Android.

LINK: https://dl.bookfunnel.com/7ezbcfai35

Manufactured by Amazon.ca
Acheson, AB